PARANORMAL

JACK WOLFSBLUME

WAVERLEY BOOKS

This edition published 2011 by Waverley Books,
144 Port Dundas Road,
Glasgow G4 0HZ

Reprinted 2011

A catalogue entry for this book is available from the British Library.

ISBN 978-1-84934-086-1

Printed and bound in Europe

CONTENTS

Chapter 4

EARTH MYSTERIES

Stonehenge and Other Stone Circles • The Druids •
Ley Lines • Dowsing • Astro-Archaeology • The Nazca
Lines • Fairy Paths • Silbury Hill • Chalk Figures and
Hill Figures • Cup and Ring Marks • Seahenge

Chapter 5

EXTRATERRESTRIALS

The Coming of the Saucers • The Roswell 'UFO' Crash
• UFOs Before the Saucers • UFO 'Waves' • Identified
Flying Objects • Space Brothers, Contactees and Alien
Abductions • Other Encounters with Aliens • Ancient
Astronauts • Crop Circles • The Min Min Lights •
Unidentified Submersible Objects • Are 'They' Here?

BIBLIOGRAPHY

INTRODUCTION

There is a view that the paranormal does not exist – that indeed the very concept of 'the paranormal' is a false one. In this view, the paranormal is either 'real' or 'not real'. If it is the latter, then it belongs in the same bag as mythology, fantasy and imagination, and we should see it as mere entertainment rather than a way to understand some of the puzzling aspects of the world. And if the paranormal is genuine, then it is not *para*normal at all but *normal*, part of our everyday, rational, scientifically approved world.

If only things were so simple. As you will discover in the following pages, some paranormal powers, such as dowsing, emotional telepathy, and (perhaps) psychokinesis, appear to have an objective reality, even though their authenticity is confined to a very small number of cases. But if such powers are truly real, we do not have the slightest clue how they work or where they fit into the spectrum of known science. And while some areas of the paranormal are almost certainly fake or fantasy (psychic surgery and alien abduction come to mind here), other subjects, such as precognition, contact with the dead and mediumship, are very much in the 'might be real/might not be real' category. Then when you come to debate the reality or otherwise of a number of mysterious beings across the world, from the Himalayan Yeti to the American Bigfoot, the mist of confusion really comes down. And the very question 'What is real?' is made much more difficult to answer by the actions of hoaxers, daydreamers, charlatans and frauds, sometimes with the enthusiastic participation of the mass media. So if you *know* exactly what is 'real', you are doing better than most of us.

The simple fact is that our world is very, very complex. Scientists exploring the depths of the universe or peering into the subatomic world are finding amazing and strange things every day. Psychologists and anthropologists are continuously uncovering bizarre and exotic forms of human behaviour and thinking. And the natural world, from the depths of the oceans to the jungles of the tropics, is constantly revealing new wonders, new species and new ecologies. We live in a world of wonders, many of which were once thought to be impossible. In the 18th century, astronomers declared that meteorites did not exist; the hundreds of pieces of space rock in the world's museums rather disprove that these days. Not that long ago, biologists asserted that all life was carbon-based. Now we know of bacteria on our own planet that consume sulphur to live – a process once thought to be impossible. Who knows, tomorrow an explorer may bring back proof of a living dinosaur from the jungle swamps of Central Africa, or new forensic technology will finally reveal the identity of Kasper Hauser. Physicists are already seriously contemplating the reality of parallel dimensions, matter transmission and time travel.

In this world of rapidly increasing knowledge, the paranormal exists partly in shadow. In some cases what was once just a piece of folklore enters the light of respectability – poltergeist phenomena, for instance, are now being treated more seriously by researchers with proper scientific credentials. But in other areas, the subject remains beyond the pale – you won't find many scientists taking ley lines seriously, for example. So the word 'paranormal' remains useful, although its meaning is fluid: what used to be regarded as paranormal yesterday may today be granted scientific recognition, or it may simply be chucked on the intellectual scrapheap.

This book explores some of the main areas of the paranormal, from mysterious sightings (of animals, people and even islands), to the inter-related fields of parapsychology and the spirit world, the jumble of ancient puzzles known as earth mysteries, and strange things that have been seen in the sky, from phantom airships in Victorian times to the 'alien invasion fleets' of today. Join us as we venture into the deserts of South America, the stone circles of Britain, and the laboratories of universities – not to mention the séance room, the gulfs of interstellar space, and the unexplored regions of the human mind.

Chapter 1

MYSTERIOUS SIGHTINGS

Human beings have been seeing strange and unexplained things since before the dawn of history. Mysterious people appear as if out of nowhere, the sky (and sometimes the earth) seems to be alive with enigmatic lights, objects perform manoeuvres that seem to defy the laws of physics, and the world of nature offers up encounters with apparently impossible creatures. In the latter case, cryptozoologists (those who research unknown or mysterious animals) often use the generic term 'cryptids' to describe the objects of their investigations.

THE LOCH NESS MONSTER

The most famous cryptid in Britain, if not the world, is the beast that is said to live in the deep dark waters of Loch Ness. Affectionately known as Nessie, the Loch Ness Monster is generally referred to as 'she', although there has never been an opportunity for anyone to determine the sex of this mythical creature. Nessie attracts visitors from all over the world – tourists, reporters and scientific investigators – and over the years she has been subjected to more camera surveillance than any 'reality TV' programme participant is ever likely to have to endure. In spite of this, she remains elusive, guarding her privacy carefully in the hidden murky depths of the loch, rewarding the thousands of hopeful spectators who come to see her with no more than the occasional tantalising glimpse of what she might, or might not, look like.

The first written record of a beast in the Loch Ness area is in Saint Adamnan's biography of Saint Columba, which was written in the 7th century. According to Adamnan, Saint Columba was walking along the shore of the River Ness in AD 565 when he caught sight of an enormous creature in the water just about to attack a man who was swimming there (the River Ness drains out of the loch, meeting the sea at Inverness). Saint Columba ordered the beast to depart in the name of God, and never to harm a human being again. The creature obeyed him, and since then, so the story goes, there have been no reports of the Loch Ness Monster threatening anyone.

Over the years, the Loch Ness Monster seems to have surfaced from time to time, giving rise to a number of stories about the beast in the loch, but it was only in the 20th century that Nessie's name came to real prominence. In the 1930s, a road was built alongside the northern shore of the loch. This brought a growth in the number of people visiting the area and also afforded passers-by a clear view of the loch from their cars. In 1933, Nessie hit the headlines of the *Inverness Courier*. A couple who lived in the district claimed to have seen an enormous creature thrashing about in the surface waters of the loch. The article in the *Courier* marked the beginning of Nessie's meteoric rise to fame. It was not long before she had allegedly been sighted on land – casually crossing the road by the loch one day in early summer. Loch Ness Monster fever rapidly spread and Nessie often became a national headline as groups of people swarmed to the shores of Loch Ness hoping to see, or catch, the creature who dwelt therein. In August of that year, when the fever was at its peak, there were no less than nine alleged sightings of the monster in the water. In July 1934, there were at least eight more. Less than a year later, however, the first wave of monster-hunting began to peter out after some plaster casts of large animal footprints, which were said to belong to the monster, were exposed as hoaxes. How many of the claimed sightings were also fake?

In spite of the scepticism of many, interest in the possibility of a mysterious creature dwelling in the loch did not go away entirely. Sightings continued to be reported from time to time in the years that followed, and in the 1960s monster fever seemed to take a hold of the public imagination once again. With the resurgence in public interest came another increase in the number of alleged sightings. The summer of 1966 was particularly busy. The 1970s and 1980s seem to have been a time of general cynicism, or short-sightedness, for scarcely a handful of sightings were recorded, but from the 1990s onwards, armed with sophisticated photography equipment, video cameras, etc., members of the public took up the hunt once more.

So, if the Loch Ness Monster does exist, or has ever existed, what sort of creature might she be? In the days of Saint Columba, she was seen (or imagined) to be one of the kelpies or water-horses – mythical creatures which were believed to prey on unsuspecting human victims, particularly children, luring them onto their backs before dragging them down into the water, never to be seen again. In more recent times, she has been described as having between one and three humps, which are somewhere between 4 and 40 feet in length and are commonly said to resemble an upturned boat. People who claim to have seen her say she has a long tail and a long neck (around 6 feet long) and a mouth that is approximately a foot wide. When submerging and moving off, she makes a great splash and leaves a v-shaped wake behind her.

Of course although the creature is commonly referred to as the Loch Ness Monster (singular), it cannot be possible that there has only been one creature surviving nearly 1,500 years since the days of Saint Columba. There must have been, at least, a succession of breeding pairs over the centuries, and the fact that on a few occasions not one, but two 'monster wakes' have allegedly been spotted simultaneously, seems to support this theory. The one identifiable creature which Nessie can be said to resemble most closely is the plesiosaur, which was a carnivorous marine reptile of the Jurassic and Cretaceous periods. Plesiosaurs could grow to around 40 feet in length, had long necks and turtle-shaped bodies, with paddle-like flippers to propel themselves through the water. There are many people who believe that Nessie is a plesiosaur, and, although the survival of a family of such creatures in one isolated place in Scotland is hard to explain when all the others became extinct 65 million years ago, there have been attempts to demonstrate that such a thing is possible. One notion suggests that some plesiosaur eggs, long frozen in the deep, cold recess of the loch, could have thawed out and hatched to start the new dynasty. The sceptics, however, point out that the loch is a low-nutrient environment: quite simply, the loch does not have an adequate supply of food for *any* large animal, never mind a 'monster'.

Loch Ness is huge, dark, and deep, a challenging environment not only for all those who wish to prove Nessie's existence but also for those who wish to disprove it. The mystery is kept at the forefront of the public's imagination with boat trips and sightseeing tours around the loch on offer to visiting tourists, and two Loch Ness Monster Exhibitions in the village of Drumnadrochit. Alleged sightings are faithfully recorded in detail, and video footage of gloomy, unidentifiable shapes in the water is studied closely by enthusiasts and sceptics alike. For the real Nessie fan, the opportunity to look for the monster via a webcam, from the comfort of their own home, has taken the hunt into the 21st century. The legend continues to grow.

OTHER LAKE MONSTERS

Nessie may be the most famous freshwater cryptid in the world, but reports of lake monsters are found in all of the earth's continents (apart from Antarctica) and right back through time. The indigenous peoples of America and Canada have numerous stories of dangerous lake-dwelling beasties, and indeed two of the most celebrated New World monsters are 'Champ', the monster of Lake Champlain in Vermont, and 'Ogopogo', the Lake Okanagan monster (in British Columbia, Canada). Some Australian Aboriginal accounts of lake-dwelling 'bunyips' may be mythological in nature, but detailed reports from the country's early colonial period have led some researchers to suggest that the stories are based on deep memories of diprodonts, now-extinct giant marsupials. But if bunyips are exclusively legendary in nature, this does not explain recent sightings by both Westerners and Aboriginals. From the 16th century onwards, observers in France, Germany, Switzerland, Italy, Scandinavia and Siberia were reporting lake-dwelling 'dragons' or similar creatures. During the Victorian period there was a well-organised attempt to net a water-horse in a loch on the Isle of Skye. In the 1920s, the 'Patagonian plesiosaur' attracted attention in Argentina, while Bolivia's Lake Titicaca is also supposedly home to some kind of unknown creature. The 1940s saw an unsuccessful hunt for the *Buru* in Assam, India. In more recent years there have been flurries of monster-spotting activity at Lake Seljordsvatnet in Norway, Lake Storsjön in Sweden, Lough Dubh in County Galway, Ireland, Lake Tana in Ethiopia, the lakes of Tasek Bera and Tasek Chini in Malaysia, Lake Hanas in China, and the Javanese Lake Patenggang.

Closer to home, there have been some intriguing but inconclusive accounts from Lake Windermere and Lake Bassenthwaite in the Lake District, as well as Loch Garten and Loch Oich in Scotland. But, excluding Nessie, the best recorded lake cryptid in Britain is the monster affectionately dubbed 'Morag'.

As with Nessie, this creature is familiarly referred to as female and she supposedly dwells hundreds of feet below the surface of Loch Morar on the wild west coast of Scotland. The loch is not as large in surface area as Loch Ness but its waters are much deeper. Morag has not reached the same dizzy heights of stardom as

Nessie, and her history is not as long, but for those who are fascinated with mythical creatures of the deep, the possibility of her existence is no less exciting.

The earliest recorded sightings of the Loch Morar Monster date from the second half of the 19th century. From time to time, fishermen out on the loch, or walkers making their way along its rocky shores, would claim to have seen one or more dark humps in the water, like upturned boats. Superstitions about death and dying were still very much a part of life in the Highlands in those days, and some said that these strange sights were omens of death, ghostly boats that warned of some tragedy to come. Others were not so sure, for they were convinced that the humps were a part of something living, some mysterious creature that rarely allowed itself to be seen. Years passed, and the rumours of the creature slowly grew.

Many of the people who claimed to have seen Morag were fishing on the loch at the time. The sight of her hump (or humps) appearing and disappearing in the water has caused great perplexity to a number of people over the years. In the 1960s, Morag was allegedly responsible for ruining an entire day's fishing for two young men. They were rowing out into the loch, and saw what they thought was a smooth, rounded rocky outcrop sticking out of the water, so they started to navigate their way round the obstacle with care. Their boat was hired, and they had no wish to pay for any damages they might incur with a careless bump. They were only half way round this miniature island when it suddenly moved, then sank, bumping into their little boat on the way down and making ripples of such a size that they almost capsized. Forgetting all about fishing, or the price they had paid for a day's boat hire, the two young men rowed back to shore as quickly as possible. There, with wide eyes and white faces, they returned the boat to its puzzled owner, muttering as they did so about the dangers 'out there'.

Descriptions of Morag, who has been seen mostly in the water, but also, on at least one occasion, on shore, make her sound very similar in appearance to the alleged creature from Loch Ness. She is dark in colour – brownish-black or black. Her skin is bumpy, like that of a reptile. She has been variously described as having one, two, three or four humps, and it is thought that she is around 30 feet long. Like Nessie, she has a long neck. One man who claimed to have seen her also said that he found her footprints in some soft ground on the shore, and they were diamond-shaped. A monster spotter with artistic leanings, Dr. George Cooper, painted her portrait in 1958, but as Morag rarely reveals more of herself than a hump here and a neck there, it is hard to tell whether Dr. Cooper managed to capture a true likeness. Those who have the time, energy and enthusiasm to continue the search will maybe be rewarded one day with the chance to see Morag for themselves.

Loch Morar is more remote and less easily accessible than Loch Ness and, most of the time, Morag is left in peace. Every now and then, another alleged sighting is logged in the records of keen cryptozoologists, but most visitors to the area barely give her more than a passing thought, and her presence is not advertised. For those who live close to Loch Morar, it is probably a good thing that Morag has not drawn the same attention to herself as Nessie. There is no monster exhibition, and local people are, for the most part, reluctant to exploit the monster rumours in any way. But monster enthusiasts are a die-hard bunch, and for them the legend lives on, even if it breathes more quietly than the legend of Nessie. And the notions about what she might be are much the same: like Nessie, she is imagined as being plesiosaur-like.

On a lighter note, it has even been suggested that far, far underground, there is a long water-filled tunnel that connects Loch Ness with Loch Morar and that the Loch Ness Monster and the Loch Morar Monster are one and the same creature, travelling between the two sites. Presumably this 60-mile-long tunnel has been overlooked by centuries of geographical exploration, although more realistically it is the kind of enjoyably silly story that lake monsters attract. We quite like the idea that, in the way that all film stars do, Nessie sometimes tires of all the cameras and attention, and at times like these, we might imagine that she takes a break from life in Loch Ness and goes to Loch Morar to annoy a few fishermen for a change.

THE *MOKELE-MBEMBE* – A LOST DINOSAUR?

With scientific analysis showing that Nessie cannot be a plesiosaur, the best place to find a living remnant of the Age of Dinosaurs might prove to be the vast unexplored swamps around Lake Tele in what is now the Republic of Congo. For many years the Likouala Pygmies from this remote area of central West Africa have talked about a large reptile-like creature they call the *mokele-mbembe*, which translates as 'the one who stops the flow of rivers'.

The creature is described as having a very long neck and tail, a small head, and a reddish-brown body the size of an elephant, standing on four thick but stubby legs. This is an almost exact description of the herbivorous sauropod dinosaurs from the Jurassic Era (200–145 million years ago), and indeed when shown pictures of various animals the Pygmies have said the *mokele-mbembe* resembles the giant plant-eaters of that period such as *Diplodocus* or *Apatosaurus* (the latter being the contemporary name for the dinosaur that used to be called *Brontosaurus*).

The incredibly hostile terrain makes exploration difficult and despite studies in the area by several scientific expeditions, no reliable evidence has been forthcoming. There are, however, some intriguing observations from the colonial period. In the 1770s French missionaries reported seeing a set of enormous clawed tracks, each print around 3 feet in circumference. The German-run Likouala-Congo Expedition of 1913 collected numerous native reports of the *mokele-mbembe*, and a reference to a persistent local belief in a creature called the *mbokale-muembe* was reported by a German magistrate in 1938. Even more astonishing, the 1913 expedition turned up references to another mysterious dinosaur-like creature, the *emela-ntouka*, which had a typical sauropod long neck, but a small head topped by a large horn. Recent researchers have speculated that the *emela-ntouka* may be an example of what is called sexual dimorphism – perhaps male *mokele-mbembes* have horns, while females do not. On the other hand, it is possible that a cluster of different but related species is present.

In 1980 and 1981 Professor Roy P. Mackal from

the University of Chicago led two expeditions into the area, logging numerous eye-witness sightings from local people from the 1960s onwards, most filled with consistent details about the appearance and behaviour of the alleged dinosaur-like beast. Although it was sometimes seen on land, the vast majority of the sightings suggested the creature preferred an aquatic or swampy environment (which accords with what fossils can tell us about the behaviour of the giant sauropod dinosaurs). Most witnesses said the 'water dragon' spent most of its time fully submerged, occasionally thrusting its head and neck above the surface to feed on vegetation.

As described in his book, *A Living Dinosaur? In Search of Mokele-Mbembe*, on one occasion Mackal and his team were travelling in dugout canoes along the Likouala-aux-Herbes River when they came within a few seconds of a direct encounter with the creature. They heard a great 'plop' and saw a large wave created by something that had entered the water beside a shadow-darkened riverbank. The pygmies screamed '*Mokele-mbembe! Mokele-mbembe!*' and only returned to the spot with great reluctance, by which time there was no sign of the cause of the water disturbance. Mackal, however, noted that crocodiles do not create such waves, elephants cannot submerge entirely (they need to keep their trunk above water) and the only alternative animal of the right size, the hippo, did not live in the Likouala swamps. In his opinion, he had been just a few yards away from a living dinosaur.

Further expeditions in the 1980s and 1990s revealed tantalising glimpses of the mysterious creature, but came no nearer to providing solid evidence for its existence. At one point cryptozoologists were shown trails of trampled vegetation said to be where the *mokele-mbembe* had entered the water, but no biological samples or photographs have been forthcoming. One of the key reasons for this is that the swamplands are among the most difficult and dangerous environments on earth.

The Likouala region of the Republic of Congo is also home to reports of a giant snake-like cryptid called a *nguma-monene* and the triple-named *mbielu-mbielu-mbielu*, a monster with 'plates' growing out of its back like the Jurassic stegosaurus dinosaur. Giant reptiles similar to *mokele-mbembe* have also been reported from other countries in central, east and west Africa, including Cameroon, the Democratic Republic of the Congo (formerly Zaire), where the local name is *irizima*, Gabon (home of the *n'yamala*), Zambia, where it is known as the *isiququmadevu*, and the Central African Republic, where the creature is variously known as the *badigui*, *diba*, *guaneru*, *ngakula-ngu* and *songo*. Meanwhile the *mbilintu* or *chipekwe*, described as either a large rhinoceros-like creature or yet another long-necked sauropod-like dinosaur, has been reported from Lake Bangweulu and Lake Mweru in Zambia, Lake Tanganyika in Tanzania, and the swamps of the Democratic Republic of the Congo. Between them these countries cover many thousands of square miles, with extensive bands of inhospitable swamplands that may possibly be ideal 'dinosaur' territory.

The *mokele-mbembe* had a brief moment of Hollywood fame in the film *Baby: Secret of the Lost Legend*, in which a palaeontologist discovers an annoyingly cute infant dinosaur in the African jungle.

Despite all the attention, however, nothing can be said for certain concerning Africa's 'mystery monsters'. The extinction horizon for the dinosaurs was 64 million years ago – can it be possible that some species survived that cataclysmic event and continue to thrive in Africa's humid swamps? Or are people seeing unrecognised versions of modern animals, such as a giant species of monitor lizard that has not been previously classified by science? Several large species have been discovered in remote regions over the past hundred years, including the Komodo dragon, the megamouth shark and the Vu Quang ox – so it is entirely possible that unknown megafauna await discovery in the vast biodiversity of the African swamplands. But will they turn out to be dinosaurs?

SEA SERPENTS

It's not just freshwater bodies of water that are associated with strange creatures: the far more extensive, and far less explored, realm of the oceans also throws up many a monster. And, some would say, the sheer size and diversity of the planet's marine environment means that sea monsters are, compared to their lake-dwelling cousins, far more plausible creatures.

In the 16th century, the Swedish bishop, Olaus Magnus, wrote a description of the northern European world that included several mentions of sea serpents and other marine monsters. Some time before the 1750s, a multi-humped creature was spotted by several witnesses off the Norwegian coast, while another bizarre sight was logged by a ship off western Greenland in 1734. As the shipping lanes got busier from the

Age of Exploration to the Age of Industry, so too did eye-witness reports of encounters with bizarre, even gigantic, aquatic animals. Many of these encounters took place within North American waters.

One famous early example was the Gloucester sea serpent, witnessed by multiple denizens of Gloucester Harbour, Massachusetts, between 1817 and 1820. Dark-brown or black, with multiple vertical humps (which means it cannot be a snake-like creature, as reptiles cannot move their spine in this way), it was described as being 65 feet in length, and capable of outpacing the fastest ship. A similarly sinuous cryptid was spotted north of San Francisco in 1983, and again in San Francisco Bay two years later. And in 1934 a long serpentine beast was seen by several witnesses – including a pair of duck hunters and the local magistrate – on South Pender Island on Canada's west coast.

Another Canadian sea serpent is known as 'Caddy', after Cadboro Bay off British Columbia, the scene of its regular sightings (the local Chinook Indians in the area have long called the creature by the delightfully euphonious name of *hiachuckaluck*). It is described as having a very elongated body that frequently undulates in 'humps', a camel-like head atop a cobra-esque 'neck', and something that looks like spikes along its spine. Observers have estimated its length as anything from 16 feet to over 100 feet. Sightings date back to at least 1897, with significant encounters throughout the 20th century, including two pilots who spotted a pair of Caddies from the air in 1993. There was even a spate of reports from 1933, the year the Loch Ness Monster went global. In 1937 an alleged Caddy carcass was found inside the belly of a sperm whale. It was badly decomposed, and may have been anything from a basking shark to a whale foetus. Almost 60 years later a pair of cryptozoologists re-examined the photographs of the mangled body and suggested it was some kind of plesiosaur that had evolved over the past 60 million years into a creature related to, but different from, the sea monsters of the dinosaur era. They even suggested a scientific name for the reptile – *Cadborosaurus* – but it is fair to say that most researchers think Caddy may be some kind of marine mammal, because, as described above, reptiles cannot undulate vertically – which is what several witnesses describe Caddy as doing.

In 1877 an alligator-like monster some 60 feet long was seen in the mid-Atlantic, with a similar cryptid spotted off the Brazilian coast in 1901. Something that sounds like the same kind of crocodilian monster was described off the Cook Islands in the Pacific in 1993.

In British waters, a long-necked sea serpent was spotted off the Orkney Islands in 1910, while on several separate occasions in 1872 a number of reliable witnesses saw a serpentine creature some 60 feet long in Loch Hourn and the Sound of Sleat, on the west coast of Scotland. The Rev. John McRae, Minister of Glenelg, and the Rev. David Twopeny, Vicar of Stockbury in Kent, described their experience in the authoritative journal *Zoology*:

> 'While we were looking at it with our glasses another similar black lump rose to the left of the first, leaving an interval between; then another and another followed, all in regular order. We did not doubt its being one living creature: it moved slowly across our wake,

and disappeared. Presently the first mass, which was evidently the head, reappeared, and was followed by the rising of the other black lumps, as before. Sometimes three appeared, sometimes four, five, or six, and then sank again. When they rose, the head appeared first, if it had been down, and the lumps rose after it in regular order, beginning always with that next the head, and rising gently; but when they sank, they sank altogether rather abruptly, sometimes leaving the head visible.'

More recently, Falmouth Bay in Cornwall has had several reports of a long-necked and humped creature dubbed 'Morgawr' (which means 'sea giant' in the Cornish language). One witness in 1976 described it as 'a sort of prehistoric dinosaur thing, with a neck the length of a lamppost'. There were more sightings that same year, along with one in 1985 witnessed by a trained scientific observer, who watched an animal some 17 to 20 feet long swimming gracefully on the surface for several minutes, before it abruptly submerged vertically.

So are sea serpents genuine animals? Quite possibly, yes. Although they are unlikely to be *serpents* – that is, reptiles – their existence as marine megafauna is not impossible according to current scientific knowledge. Although their size has probably been exaggerated by witnesses (it is notoriously difficult to estimate length over the surface of the sea) there is a good chance that a small number of large, unknown species remain to be discovered in the world's oceans. It is therefore worth finishing this section with a quotation from the classic examination of monstrous cryptids, *Mythical Monsters*, published by investigator Charles Gould in 1886:

> 'In conclusion, I must strongly express my own conviction, which I hope, after the perusal of the evidence contained in the foregoing pages, will be shared by my readers, that, let the relations of the sea-serpent be what they may; let it be serpent, saurian, or fish, or some form intermediate to them; and even granting that those relations may never be determined, or only at some very distant date; yet, nevertheless, the creature must now be removed from the regions of myth, and credited with having a real existence, and that its name includes not one only, but probably several very distinct gigantic species, allied more or less closely, and constructed to dwell in the depths of the ocean, and which only occasionally exhibit themselves to a fortune-favoured wonder-gazing crew.'

MAN-BEASTS

In man-beasts, we have the cryptids that appear to be the closest to us, a variety of largely bipedal ape-like creatures reported from many of the world's less developed areas. Among their number are cryptozoological celebrities, such as Bigfoot and the Yeti, while the category also includes lesser-known cryptids along the lines of the Almas of Mongolia, the Yeren of China, and the Sasquatch of Canada. From their appearance there is the assumption that the beings are primates, that is, of the same group as humans, apes and monkeys, and they are sometimes also called 'manimals', 'ape-men', and 'BHMs' (big hairy men). No-one, however, has produced definitive proof that any of these critters exist. Folklore, superstition, misidentification and hoaxing certainly play a part in the story of some of these man-beasts, but they remain perhaps the most fascinating group of cryptids on the planet.

The Yeti

On 8 November 1951, Eric Shipton, Michael Ward and a Sherpa, Sen Tensing, encountered a line of footprints stretching for a mile through the snow at 18,000 feet, on the approaches to Mount Everest. The prints were of a bipedal creature – that is, it walked on its hind legs like a human – and were so huge that the estimated height of the creature was some 8 feet. The photographs Shipton took of the prints caused a sensation. For some, this was the best proof yet of the existence of the legendary man-ape of the Himalayas, the Yeti (known in the West by the faintly ridiculous title of the Abominable Snowman). More sceptical commentators noted that footprints can become enlarged and distorted as snow melts and refreezes, and that the tracks were probably of a mountain bear. And, under unusual conditions, simulacra of what appear to be footprints can spontaneously appear in snow. The prints were intriguing and strange, but they did not constitute proof of the Yeti's existence.

More mysterious Himalayan footprints were recorded in 1954. Then in 1970 British mountaineer, Don Williams, had a clear sighting of a large ape-like creature at a height of 13,000 feet. Unfortunately he was unable to use his camera at the time, although he had been photographing the snow-tracks of an unknown animal earlier that day. Many accounts of the Yeti or *meh-te* ('man-beast') have been collected from local people in Tibet and Nepal. The Abbot of Thyangboche Monastery, for example, saw a 5-foot-tall hairy biped playing in the snow, before it was driven off by Buddhist monks blowing bugles and conch shells. The general consensus was that adult Yetis had reddish-brown fur, stood about 6 feet 6 inches tall, and had a largely hairless face with a pronounced ridge or crest along the skull. They lived on fruit and vegetation, had no language, and tended to avoid humans.

Several pieces of physical evidence have come to light in monasteries, unfortunately none of them definitive. The bones of an alleged Yeti paw (or hand) were examined *in situ* by Western scientists and declared to belong to an unknown primate, but the relic was stolen in 1991. Two alleged mummified corpses in Tibetan monasteries may well have been destroyed or stolen during the military annexation of the country by China. And several so-called Yeti scalps have proved to be just the skin of a mountain antelope – although, in fairness, the monks have always maintained that these were *representations* of Yeti scalps, worn during ceremonies in which participants take on the role of the Yeti. Meanwhile, DNA analysis of an alleged Yeti hair sample collected in 2001 has revealed it belonged to an unknown creature.

Overall, there is a reasonable chance that a large unknown animal, possibly a primate, may well be dwelling among the snowy wastes of the Himalayas.

The Yeren and Almas

The Yeren or 'Chinese wild man' is a 6-foot-tall hairy biped reported from the Shennongjia Mountains in central China. It is described as having reddish hair, sunken eye sockets and a protruding jaw. A forestry worker had a clear sighting of one in 1977, and a specimen was allegedly shot in 1940 (although the corpse has since disappeared). Stories of hairy ape-men dwelling in China's more remote regions go back to at least the 16th century, but at this remove it is difficult to distinguish fact from folklore.

The Almas (the word is singular, plural Alma) is a hairy humanoid biped said to be found in Mongolia and the Central Asian areas of Russia. It is also known as the Kaptar or Almasty, both words meaning 'forest man'. Like the Yeren, it is supposed to be muscular, long-armed and covered in reddish-grey hair. A scientist from Leningrad University had a clear sighting of one on two separate occasions in 1957. Another scientist saw a similar creature in 1978. Reports from both local people and Russians in Mongolia during the 1970s even suggest the Alma exhibit human-like behaviours, using stone tools to kill and butcher animals for clothing and food.

This has led several commentators to suggest that the Almas is an early form of the genus *Homo*, possibly a distant ancestor like *Homo erectus*, or an ancestor of *Homo neanderthalis* (Neanderthal man), or even an otherwise unknown relative of ourselves (we are *Homo sapiens*). Others speculate that the Almas could belong to a relict population of *Gigantopithecus*, an extinct giant ape-like creature known from fossils 100,000 years old.

Man-beasts are reported from much of Asia. In Siberia they are called the Chuchunaa ('outcast'). The Iranian version is the Nasnas ('wild man') or Dev ('demon'). Pakistan has the Bar-manu ('big hairy one'). The Kaptar allegedly lurks in the Caucasus. The Orang Dalam (the so-called 'Malay Bigfoot') was allegedly seen as recently as 2006. Sumatra has the Orang Pendek, Borneo the Batutut, and Sri Lanka the Nittaewo. There are sightings from Sikkim, Assam and Bangladesh.

Further afield, a smaller ape-man called the Agogwe is claimed for Tanzania and neighbouring African countries. The Mapinguary from the Amazon rainforest of Brazil may be another of these mystery ape-men, although recent research suggests it might be an unknown species of giant ground-dwelling sloth. Hairy men called Woodwuses or Wodewoses were mentioned in several early European accounts: if they were ever real beings and not just figures of folklore, they were probably exterminated by the 17th century.

The Yeti, Yeren, Almas and their kin may be the same animal, or entirely unrelated – that is, if they exist at all. Sadly no reliable scientific evidence has been forthcoming that establishes objectively and with certainty the existence of the Central Asian ape-men, although a British expedition in 2009 claimed a close encounter on the verandah of a semi-derelict building – but, once again, there was no physical or photographic proof.

The Minnesota Iceman

This is one of the most intriguing – and frustrating – of modern man-beasts. In the 1960s, a travelling showman from Minnesota, Frank Hansen, exhibited a hairy bipedal creature in a block of ice. Hansen claimed that the specimen was a modern Neanderthal who had been shot in Vietnam, hinting that this had been during the American military presence in the country and that the corpse had been brought back to the USA in a body bag. In 1968 two experienced cryptozoologists, Ivan T. Sanderson and Dr. Bernard Heuvelmans, examined the creature within its icy tomb, and took a series of photographs. The images show an ape-like man covered in dark hair everywhere except on the face and palms of the hands. Although they were unable to handle the corpse itself, in the opinion of the two scientists, the specimen was genuine.

If the Minnesota Iceman was indeed a bona fide Asian man-beast then the implications for cryptozoology – and for science in general – are immense. Sadly, however, the full battery of modern biological technology, from DNA analysis to techniques that can determine the diet and geographical home of an individual, cannot help us. For reasons unknown, Hansen substituted a replica, and the whereabouts of the original specimen are unknown. It may even have been destroyed. We will probably never know whether it was a real cryptid, or a clever fake.

Bigfoot and Sasquatch

The most famous cryptid on the North American continent, Bigfoot, is a staple of popular culture (as in the movie *Bigfoot and the Hendersons*). Bigfoot hunting is potentially big business, with a variety of colourful characters vying with each other to obtain *the* perfect photograph or piece of physical evidence. Anyone who turns up with indisputable proof of Bigfoot's existence stands to make a lot of money; in such a commercial atmosphere it is perhaps not surprising that the world of 'Bigfootology' is rife with accusations of fraud and fabrication – not to mention legal disputes.

One of the earliest accounts comes from 1811, in Alberta, Canada (where one of the Indian names for the manimal is Sasquatch). Explorer David Thompson found a series of tracks 14 inches long, and since then many such tracks have been discovered – several of which have been preserved in plaster of Paris in recent times, the resulting casts clearly showing how Bigfoot got its name. (It should be noted that some reports of Bigfoot tracks have been shown to be hoaxes.) A detailed eye-witness account from an Oregon hunter in 1869 described a 5-foot-tall creature with dark brown hair, broad shoulders and short legs and a small head. The manimal used a stick and whistled, and was later joined by a female with noticeable breasts. Intriguingly, female Bigfoots are quite frequently mentioned, in complete contrast to the Asian man-beasts, which are never discussed in terms of their sex. The principal reports centre on forested areas and stretch from northern California along America's west coast through Oregon and Washington into western Canada. It has been speculated that Bigfoot's original natural range has shrunk because of the increasing population and development of the North American continent. If this is the case, perhaps Bigfoots were more common and more widespread in the days before European settlement.

Recent researchers have combed old newspapers for historical accounts of Bigfoot sightings (although there is an undeniable problem here, in that early American newspapers were notorious for printing dramatic or fantastical fake stories, often competing with each other to see who could invent the most ridiculous 'true story'). Chad Arment, in *The Historical Bigfoot*, for example, found over 100 reports across 40 American states, from Alaska to Florida, plus others in several Canadian provinces. Before 'Bigfoot' became established as a name, newspapers used terms such as 'Wild Man', 'What-Is-It', 'Yahoo' (a name derived from Jonathan Swift's *Gulliver's Travels*), 'Nondescript', 'Gorilla' and even Lewis Carroll's 'Jabberwocky' (from *Alice Through the Looking-Glass*). These reports can be very valuable because they date from a time before everyone 'knew' what Bigfoot looked like, and thus they are less contaminated by expectation. Although there is considerable variation in the historical descriptions, most contain the core information that the mystery animal was shaggy-haired, varied from the size of a small human to the height of an exceptionally tall man, and walked upright.

Sightings, claims, counterclaims and casts of footprints started to increase from the 1950s, but it was not until 1967 that Bigfoot became a national and international celebrity. That year saw what is without doubt the most sensational piece of cryptozoological footage ever filmed – the Patterson-Gimlin film, made by ranchers Roger Patterson and Bob Gimlin. Over a few seconds the piece shows a tall, black-haired manlike creature walking upright through a forest in northern California. Every frame of the film has been endlessly analysed. For some enthusiasts, it is proof positive that Bigfoot exists. For others, what looks like the head of a zip fastener on the animal's neck shows that the whole thing is a fake – a man in a special-effects monkey suit.

As if things could get any weirder, Bigfoot is increasingly associated with other strange phenomena such as UFO sightings (including abductions!), mysterious cattle mutilations and strange lights. In addition, the creature is sometimes reported as possessing red or luminous eyes, having a bulletproof hide, and the ability to move at impossible speeds without leaving tracks. This has led to suggestions that Bigfoot is not a flesh-and-blood creature, but an elemental or phantom, some kind of supernatural guardian of the great American woods. In this way Bigfoot may be an avatar of the Wendigo, a monster from Native American belief – a spirit of ice, cold and fear, said to prey on lone travellers in the forest, and a harbinger of starvation and cannibalism.

Those in search of objective evidence have collected hair samples (which DNA analysis shows to be primate in nature) and recorded alleged Bigfoot cries (whose acoustic properties could not have been made by the human larynx). In 1999 a cast was made of an impression in mud where a Bigfoot was thought to have rested. According to its supporters, the Skookum cast – named after the location in Washington State – shows the outline of the creature's entire left side from arm to foot. Not surprisingly, sceptics point out that you need the 'eye of faith' to make out these details.

So despite massive media and investigatory attention, not to mention the increased availability of cameras and advances in the quality of analytical technology, no-one has yet provided definitive, convincing proof for the existence of Bigfoot. Sadly, given America's gun culture, that proof might end up being a Bigfoot corpse riddled with a hunter's bullets.

Man-beasts have, not surprisingly, entered popular culture. 'Sasquatch' is a hairy mutant in the *X-Men* comic books and films, but the best-known man-beast of the fictional world is Chewbacca from the *Star Wars* films. 'Chewie' is a Wookie, a race of strong, tall, long-haired bipeds. In the movies, Wookies come from another planet, but morphologically we could be looking at a classic earthbound man-beast: Bigfoot in space.

The Yowie

Even by the weird standards of man-beasts, the Yowie ('dream spirit') is peculiarly bizarre. A giant gorilla-like bipedal cryptid over 7 feet tall, it is reported from Australia – a continent with no apes, monkeys or other primates apart from humans.

Reports of the creature date back to the earliest European settlement, and many Aboriginal tribes recognise the Yowie as part of the normal fauna of the Outback. One of the most striking reports comes from 1978 when a ranger from the Queensland National Parks and Wildlife Service had an unpleasant close encounter with the beast. At first, he thought he had seen a wild pig rooting for food (domesticated pigs escaped into the wild during the colonial period, and have established feral populations that can damage indigenous wildlife and ecology). But as the ranger approached he realised the creature looked more like a gorilla, with black hair covering its body, large yellow gorilla-like eyes set in a flat face, and a muscular build. The Yowie emitted a stench so awful that the ranger vomited, at which point the creature escaped quickly through the trees. It is interesting to note that Bigfoot and another North American cryptid known as the Skunk Ape are both said to give off terrible smells when disturbed.

If the Yowie is real, then it presents a challenge to biology, simply because Australia's wildlife, being cut off from other continents for so long, has evolved along its own path. The vast majority of its native animals are marsupials, a grouping in which the young are born very underdeveloped and then fed and raised in a pouch (mammals elsewhere are called placentals, because the foetus is nourished from the placenta inside the mother's body). The kangaroo and its joey are the most famous example of a marsupial. If the Yowie exists, it is almost certainly a marsupial, which begs the question of its ape-like appearance in a continent without apes. It is possible that the process of *convergent evolution* has resulted in an animal that *looks like* the placental apes of Africa and Asia, but is in fact a marsupial that occupies the same ecological niche. Convergent evolution has produced other parallels in Australia, such as the thylacine, an extinct marsupial that looked like the placental wolf of Europe and North America.

The Big Grey Man of Ben Macdhui

To conclude this section, let's look at what is claimed to be a home-grown man-beast – the Big Grey Man of Ben Macdhui. Ben Macdhui is the highest peak in the Cairngorms, and the second highest mountain in Scotland. From its summit, the climber is afforded a magnificent panorama of the surrounding peaks: Cairngorm, Ben Avon and Cairn Toul. To the north west, the River Spey passes through Aviemore on its way to the Moray Firth. To the east, the Dee flows towards Ballater, Aboyne and Aberdeen. The mountain is popular with climbers who visit the region from many different countries, and its slopes offer a number of routes that are both challenging and rewarding, even to experienced mountaineers. But Ben Macdhui is well known not only for its beauty and the sport that it offers its visitors. For over a century now, there has been much speculation that there may be something frightening lurking on Ben Macdhui. Over this period, several climbers claim to have witnessed a mysterious presence on the mountain; many believe it to be a physical one. This presence has been named *Am Fear Liath Mor*, more commonly known as the Big Grey Man.

On remote mountain slopes, far from the noise and bustle of centres of population, it is easy to give free rein to the imagination and let the mind wander to strange apparitions and monsters. There are plenty of things that the mountain climber encounters to provide fuel for the mind's journey; strange echoes in gullies, tricks of the light, shapes in the mist, ominous shadows cast as the sun moves across the unfamiliar landscape. Human beings are social animals, and solitude is alien to most of us. It can alter one's perceptions, especially in an unfamiliar environment, and fear of real, physical and recognisable danger can find itself accompanied by a fear of unidentifiable, intangible threats, which come from a realm far removed from man's knowledge of the physical world and its nature.

The Big Grey Man of Ben Macdhui, like the other monstrous apparitions, has allegedly been seen and heard on a number of different occasions. But there is another more sinister aspect to the Grey Man, which the other apparitions do not share. The Big Grey Man's presence is not perceived by the physical senses alone. It can make itself felt in a manner that is generally claimed to be very disturbing. It is alleged that the Grey Man exerts a strong psychic influence upon those who encounter him. And several climbers, having undergone such an encounter, have been reluctant to return to the mountain.

The first time the possible existence of the Big Grey Man of Ben Macdhui was mentioned in Scotland was in 1925. Norman Collie, a professor in Chemistry from London and an experienced and well-respected mountaineer, related his story to members of the Cairngorm Club at their Annual General Meeting. He recalled a solo climb on the mountain in 1891, and said that as he was making his way back down the mountainside from the summit through the mist, he became aware of the sound of footsteps behind him. For every three or four steps that the professor took, he heard one of these footsteps, as if whoever – or whatever – was following him was taking much larger strides than himself. At first, he dismissed the sounds as nonsense, for he could see nothing, but as he continued downwards he could still hear them. At this point he was overwhelmed by a feeling of terror, and in blind panic, took flight, descending the rest of the mountain with more concern for speed than safety on the treacherous terrain. The experience left him badly shaken, and determined that he would never climb Ben Macdhui alone again, for there was something 'very queer' about the higher slopes of the mountain.

Collie had told this story once before, some years earlier in New Zealand, and it had been greeted with a moderate degree of interest and some understandable scepticism. But when Dr. A. M. Kellas heard about it, he was more than moderately interested in Collie's experience. Dr. Kellas was another well-known figure in mountaineering circles, much respected for his achievements climbing in the Himalayas (he later died during the Everest reconnaissance expedition of 1921). When Kellas heard Collie's story, he wrote to him to tell him of his own experience. Kellas had been on Ben Macdhui with his brother, and had been hammering out crystals from some rocks quite close to the summit when they had become aware of a large figure descending from above, out of the mist. The two men had then, like Collie, succumbed to a terrible feeling of fear and been compelled to flee.

We do not know why Collie waited 34 years to tell his story to the Cairngorm Club, but it is reasonable to assume that he might have felt apprehensive about the reception it might get. Perhaps the letter from Kellas helped to give Collie the courage to relate his account of the experience they had shared. But at any rate, when he did finally speak out in 1925, he would know that there was at least one other knowledgeable, reasonable and experienced man who had testified to having had a similar encounter. Both men had spent extended amounts of time in remote mountain regions and consequently knew all too well the tricks that could be played on the mind when a person was alone, cold and tired. They were also familiar with the strange sights and sounds of such places – shadows in the mist, falling rocks, echoes and suchlike. But both strenuously denied that the phenomenon they had witnessed was anything like this.

There have been several reports of alleged encounters with the Big Grey Man since then. Some of them, undoubtedly, have been fantasy, or hoax. Others cannot be dismissed so easily. Some people claim to have heard strange voices, speaking in a foreign tongue, which has been said to resemble either Gaelic or Urdu. Others have said that they could hear hauntingly beautiful music. Alleged sightings vary from a vague description of a hazy, large, upright figure to a more precise picture of something akin to the Sasquatch or Yeti. In 1944, Captain Sir Hugh Rankin claimed to have met and spoken with the Big Grey Man on two separate occasions. According to Sir Hugh, who was a Buddhist, the Grey Man was a Bodhisattwa. (A Bodhisattwa is a being in an advanced degree of incarnation, next to that of a Buddha, who has achieved enlightenment and acts as a guide to others in their progress towards the same.) Sir Hugh was humbled, but unafraid. His experience of the Big Grey Man was apparently wholly benign.

However, most other climbers who have tales to tell of the Big Grey Man or of out-of-the-ordinary experiences on Ben Macdhui have shared feelings that are very different from those felt by Sir Hugh Rankin. Fear, sudden and overwhelming, has been commonly reported and openly admitted, even by hardened men of the outdoors. Sudden, terrible feelings of depression have also been described on a number of occasions. In some men's experience, these feelings have rapidly led to thoughts of suicide and frightening compulsions to self-harm by falling or jumping off a ledge or into a gully. This power that the phenomenon of the Grey Man seems to exert over people's minds is what makes it uniquely sinister and dangerous. Perhaps, knowing something about the phenomenon, the fear of an encounter with the Big Grey Man has both triggered and inflamed the imaginations of many climbers on the slopes of Ben Macdhui, affecting their mood and convincing them that such an encounter has taken place. But that does not explain why Collie and Kellas felt as they did, on separate occasions and quite independently of each other. Nor will all climbers since then have known about the phenomenon before they set off up the mountain.

The phenomenon may be nothing more than a collection of misperceptions, or optical and aural illusions. It may be hallucination induced by fatigue, or hysteria. Norman Collie may have had a panic attack. Dr. Kellas may have seen his own shadow in the mist. But their refusal to dismiss their experience as illusion or panic persisted until their deaths. Furthermore, there are several people still alive who claim to have experienced the Big Grey Man – whatever it is. And like Collie and Kellas, those among them whose claims were made in good faith are unlikely ever to be convinced that there is not 'something up there'.

GEF THE TALKING MONGOOSE

This case is unique in the annals of paranormal research.

Nowhere else do we find a long-term manifestation of a cryptid that, by its own spoken admission, was an Indian mongoose. Gef (pronounced 'Jeff') made his appearance in 1931 at Cashen's Gap (Doarlish Cashen in Manx) – a farm on the Isle of Man. Cashen's Gap was a working definition of the word 'isolated', being almost atop a mountain at the end of a rough track. This remote outpost was home to a former businessman turned sheep farmer, James Irving, his wife, Margaret, and daughter, Voirrey.

The case started in a mundane manner, with some kind of animal making spitting, barking and blowing noises behind the wood panelling in the house. Mr. Irving tried poison, traps and a gun, without success. So, rather bizarrely, he tried communicating with the interloper by making various animal calls. The creature imitated them. It then repeated nursery rhymes that the 13-year-old Voirrey spoke aloud. Within a few weeks it had apparently learned English, and was chattering away ten to the dozen, detailing its biography, making jokes, singing hymns and reciting pieces in Spanish, Russian and Welsh. It claimed to be an 80-year-old mongoose that had been persecuted in India. As it grew in confidence (not to say arrogance) it made demands of the household, strangled rabbits in return for its lodging, hopped on the local bus to make trips to a nearby town (where it picked up gossip it related with relish) and eventually started providing accurate clairvoyant information on people living ten miles away. Mr. Irving himself rarely saw the small, bushy-tailed creature, but Gef frequently showed himself face to face with Voirrey and Mrs. Irving. Gef even posed for Voirrey's camera, but the two resulting photographs show no sign of a mongoose, or anything else of interest.

The Cashen's Gap mongoose would have remained just a piece of local Manx weirdness had it not been for two factors: firstly, James Irving kept a diary of sorts, detailing all of Gef's manifold sayings and activities. When Gef was hungry, for example, he would say, 'Well, Jim, what about some grubbo?' And when questioned on his nature, he replied in his high-pitched voice, 'I am an earthbound spirit'. The second contribution to Gef's fame was that Irving's diary made its way to the desk of Harry Price. Price was the most famous paranormal researcher of his day. He would later investigate the notorious haunting of Borley Rectory, and popularise the use of the word 'poltergeist'.

Price thought that the case was simply too improbable to be worth investigating, but he shrewdly recognised it might have publicity value. So he sent a friend of his, Captain M. H. Macdonald, to sound out the situation. In February 1932 Macdonald visited Cashen's Gap, but saw nothing out of the ordinary. Then, as he was about to leave for the evening, he heard a high-pitched voice scream out, 'Go away! Who is that man?' The following day a large needle bounced off the teapot in front of Macdonald – he was told that Gef frequently liked to throw things. Later he heard the shrill voice again, this time upstairs. Despite his requests for Gef to appear, the voice shrieked: 'No, I don't mean to stay long, as I don't like you!' Despite his best efforts, Macdonald failed to get a sighting of the alleged mongoose.

In March 1935 Gef had been in residence for some four years. Perhaps feeling a bit ignored by the investigators, he plucked some hairs from his back and tail and instructed Mr. Irving to forward the sample to Macdonald and Price for identification. Subsequent analysis showed they had been taken from the family's collie dog. Later Macdonald visited again, and heard Gef scream and say, 'Coo-ee! Coo-ee!', although once again no visual contact was made. Then Price, in company with his friend R. S. Lambert, the editor of *The Listener* magazine, visited the farm in person (the pair later collaborated on a book entitled *The Haunting of Cashen's Gap*, and Price presented a BBC radio programme on the case). Several months before the visit, Gef had seemed to become fixated on Price, saying he did not like the investigator, stating 'He's the man who puts the kybosh on the spirits!' and that Price had 'his doubting cap on'.

Price's visit was almost a complete waste of time. Gef vanished entirely and only allegedly returned after Price and Lambert had departed. The only achievement came from Price's investigation of the house's internal geography. He determined that the runs behind the panelling in every room made the house an interconnected acoustic sounding board. 'By speaking into one of the many apertures in the panels,' he wrote, 'it should be possible to convey the voice to various parts of the house.'

What, then, was behind Gef's four-year occupation of Cashen's Gap? The obvious suggestion is that the Irving family, for some bizarre psychological reason, decided to set up an elaborate hoax in the middle of nowhere, for no financial benefit, and to maintain the illusion over several years. A more reasonable notion focuses on Voirrey. An attractive and intelligent teenage girl, she lived an isolated existence in an insular household within a farm that most observers regarded as grim and austere, if not a little forbidding. Her father was almost 60 years old, leading to a major generation gap. Perhaps she invented Gef as a means of injecting excitement into her drab life, and the project got out of hand when her duped father started taking Gef seriously, keeping a diary, and getting in touch with paranormal investigators from faraway London. It is quite possible that she was responsible for Gef's voice, the throwing of objects, and the stockpiling of Gef's strangled rabbits. Although she managed to get away with a few activities during Captain Macdonald's visit, she lost her nerve when Price, the great sceptic, came to town. Significantly, Gef deserted Cashen's Gap permanently when Voirrey left home.

However, a hoaxing hypothesis cannot easily account for the few times Gef was witnessed as a physical entity, nor can it explain the mongoose's clairvoyant knowledge of events taking place many miles away. A plausible alternative suggestion here is that Gef was a kind of poltergeist – remember, he described himself an 'earthbound spirit'. Viewed in this way, the case conforms to the classic momentum of poltergeist cases, with the phenomena starting with relatively mild noises and scratchings, progressing to the moving or throwing of objects, and finally erupting in a full-scale manifestation of multiple phenomena. Also of interest here is that when Gef started, Voirrey was a lonely girl on the brink of sexual puberty. Numerous studies of poltergeist cases have linked such outbreaks with frustrated teenagers, often girls approaching or experiencing their first period. It is as if the inner turmoil of the pubescent child is somehow expressed in an unconscious telekinetic rage. A related notion is that the disaffected teenager acts as a focus for some kind of external energy. Colin Wilson, in his study *Poltergeist!*, for example, speculated that Gef might have been an elemental or hobgoblin.

Ultimately the case of Gef the talking mongoose remains another unsolved mystery. Was it an outright hoax? A cry for help by a frustrated teenager? An expression of psychological disorder? A failed publicity stunt? Or a genuine haunting?

THE CHUPACABRAS OR 'GOATSUCKER'

Some strange phenomena seem to be very much culture-bound. The belief in witches that can make penises vanish is largely restricted to West and South Africa; only the Japanese believe that your blood group determines your love life and choice of future partner; and the Penanggalan, a flying vampiric head trailing lungs and intestines, preys only on Malaysians. And so it is with the Chupacabras, a monster that finds its home almost exclusively in the Hispanic cultures of the Caribbean, South and Central America, and the southern United States.

Unlike most cryptids in this section, the Chupacabras is a child of the internet. When reports of a bloodsucking monster started circulating in the barrios of Puerto Rico in 1995, a purely local phenomenon suddenly became an internet meme of extraordinary vitality, partly helped by numerous Spanish-language radio stations that acted as vivid channels of communication outside the mainstream Anglophone media. It also didn't hurt that the world was in the grip of *X-Files* fever (the television series went on to mention the Chupacabras, including the almost hysterical approach to the creature in some Hispanic media). In addition, it has been suggested that the Chupacabras' look was influenced by the alien monster in the science fiction horror film *Species*, which played in Puerto Rico just before the first sightings.

The Chupacabras, from the start, has been a Hispanic cryptid, and to outsiders can seem an utterly baffling phenomenon. No matter how many reports are shown to be the misinterpretation of real animals, or deliberate hoaxes, or lies (one Mexican teenager blamed the monster for 'wounds' that turned out to be lovebites from her boyfriend), the Chupacabras lives on. Every time a domestic pet goes missing, or a cow or sheep is attacked, the Chupacabras is invoked, and the victims are always said to be 'drained of blood'. Reports by the authorities that the animals have been attacked by known predators, and that exsanguination has most definitely not taken place, are routinely ignored. The 'master narrative' of the Chupacabras story is that it is an unstoppable, uncatchable vampiric monster, and any inconvenient facts that deny this story are simply brushed aside. For sociologists and folklorists, this is a 'social panic' among economically underprivileged groups; while for some people within the Hispanic community, it seems, the Chupacabras is a living, breathing monster preying on all and sundry.

The basic Puerto Rican description of the Chupacabras from 1995 has it as a grey, furred kangaroo-like beast with fierce fangs and three-clawed hands, webbed arms, and luminous or glowing spikes or feathers along its spine. As reports circulated, the creature's anatomy expanded to include wings, lidless red eyes, vampire teeth, horns, holes in the skull instead of ears, chameleon-like colour changes, and a rocking ability that makes people dizzy or nauseous. It can levitate, disappear, appear again, fly, and generally operate as a creature of magic. In a way the Chupacabras has become a catch-all monster, sucking up features and behaviours from a variety of sources – folklore, popular culture, and psychological fears. Not surprisingly for such a diverse beast, it has an equally colourful set of stories about its origin: it is said to be an extraterrestrial, an ancient pre-human predator, a mutant, a genetic experiment gone wrong, and a test subject released by the American military. Periodically a new Chupacabras 'corpse' is displayed for the delectation of the media and the excitement of the internet corps; all the specimens are either hoaxes or real animals subject to disease or decay.

It is possible that some of the cryptids in this book will turn out to be real creatures, and will join the list of scientifically recognised fauna. That will never happen for the Chupacabras: it is purely a product of the human imagination.

LOST ISLANDS

On 12 November 1764, Captain John Byron, as part of his two-year circumnavigation of the world, was at latitude 43°S off the coast of Argentina. A storm was on the horizon. What happened next was recorded in his log:

> 'All the people on the forecastle called out
> at once "Land right ahead". I looked under

the foresail and upon the lee bow, and saw it to all appearance as plain as ever I saw land in my life. It made at first like an island with two very scraggy hummocks upon it, but looking to leeward we saw the land joining it running a long way to the southwest.'

Several other officers and crew also saw and described the blue hills, and waves breaking on the sandy beaches, and were soon congratulating themselves on discovering an uncharted island. Then after about an hour, the land just disappeared. The apparently solid island completely vanished in an instant.

Byron had been at sea for 27 years, and was a vastly experienced mariner. He had never seen anything like it and stated that the entire crew would have sworn the island was utterly real. As it was, he realised that a peculiar combination of weather and viewing conditions had created the illusion of an island. It may have been a mirage, or possibly a simulacrum where clouds, rain and sea had together formed a real-seeming shape that everyone on board interpreted as a genuine island.

The episode is a perfect example that not everything seen at sea can be fully trusted. If the weather had not remained clear before the island disappeared, Byron may well have, with the full agreement of his navigator and junior officers, published the location of an entirely nonexistent island. And if you were to examine the nautical charts and atlases of the 19th century, you would find that they contained around *two hundred islands* that are entirely absent from modern cartography. Many of these 'lost islands' were simply real specks of rock poorly plotted on the charts in the days when longitude was hard to determine, and so were 'duplicates' of the actual islands many miles away. Some, such as Byron's illusory hummocked island, were the result of optical illusions brought about by the viewing environment on the vast sea. Others, however, have even stranger stories.

Let's take, for example, a whole set of tiny rocks reported in the seas off California during the 19th century. With the Gold Rush, and the growing number of trade routes across the Pacific, these waters became increasingly busy from the 1850s on and many small islands, such as the Redfield Rocks and Kentzell's Island, were reported by consecutive ships passing through the area. These islands made their way onto nautical charts and were marked as hazards to navigation. There was just one problem: they did not exist. It was not until 1902, and the advent of fully accurate surveying, that over a dozen Californian islands were finally expunged from the maps. How was it that so many experienced sailors had made false reports? Part of the explanation may rest on the sea's capacity to create optical illusions, as noted above. But another aspect may be that, once the islands were shown on the charts, they became 'real' in the minds of the mariners, and so any shadow, wave or cloudbank in the approximate position was reported as land, thus confirming the existing but false sighting.

The Californian islands were a self-perpetuating collective delusion. In a world of satellites and advanced technology we no longer 'see' nonexistent islands, but the fact is that this delusion affected many seasoned observers; you don't have to go far to find contemporary comparisons with, say, sightings of UFOs.

In some cases nonexistent islands were simply hoaxes perpetuated by their alleged discoverers. Matador Island in the Pacific, for example, was allegedly visited in 1876 by a British captain who claimed that most of the natives were albinos, and all were suffering from leprosy. Which is curious, as there were no inhabited islands in that region. Matador Island is no longer to be found on any chart. Morrell Island, northwest of Hawaii, had the advantage of being uninhabited, and therefore with no inconvenient natives for later visitors to question and compare with the alleged first encounter. But that did not make the island any less fake. Its supposed titular discoverer, Captain Benjamin Morrell, announced he had set foot on it in 1825. The American Morrell was a commercial venturer and his voyages had been financially disastrous for his backers; his invention of Morrell Island (and other fabrications in his logs) were designed to make further explorations more attractive to potential investors. A later assessment of his career described him as 'the biggest liar in the Pacific'.

Some islands, however, do genuinely appear – and then, quite often, disappear again. Typically, these are volcanic in origin, and rise above the waters following an eruption by a previously submerged volcano. At least 96 new volcanic islands appeared during the 19th and 20th centuries, most of them small additions to existing volcanic island groups. A few are permanent additions such as the island of Surtsey which erupted and rose above the seas off Iceland in 1963 and is now a nature reserve with a well-established ecology. Some subside beneath the waves again after a few years or decades. Falcon Island in the Tonga Group, for example, swung between being 'up' and 'down' at least seven times between 1865 and 1921, by which date the volcano had almost entirely disappeared. Graham's Island in the Straits of Scilly climbed to 107 feet high in 1831 before collapsing below the water level. Bogoslof Island in the Aleutians has been known to change shape and even divide into two. In 1952, Myojin Island off Japan sank beneath the surface (again) and a research vessel sailed over the submerged summit – unfortunately at the very moment that the subsea volcano erupted, leading to the loss of the ship.

One inhabited volcanic island that allegedly suffered a permanent fate was Tuanahe, a Pacific island in the Cook Group, which reportedly sank beneath the waves in 1844, taking with it its entire population. Tuanahe had never been seen by Western visitors, and the tale of its disappearance remains unconfirmed.

A different kind of fictional island was once common in the frigid southern seas around Antarctica. Over a dozen examples – including Emerald, Nimrod, Dougherty and Thompson Islands – once appeared on charts. None ever existed, and it is surmised that observers were actually seeing giant tabular icebergs several miles long, carved by the elements with simulacra of cliffs, mountains and valleys. This assumption is given credence by cases where experienced mariners realised their mistake – in 1915, for example, the *Carnegie* circumpolar expedition spotted an unknown island, but on closer approach the crew saw that what they had taken for a dark rocky mass was in fact light reflecting off an iceberg's vertical wall.

Elsewhere, lost islands are associated with the world

of legends and myth. Numerous candidates have been put forward for the location of the vanished land of Atlantis, which was supposedly an advanced ancient civilization that sank beneath the waves during a great cataclysm. Most suggestions are based in the Atlantic, and range from off the Azores to close to Bermuda; none are convincing, and current archaeological thinking leans towards the Atlantis myth being based on the volcanic destruction of the Greek island of Santorini around 1600 BC.

In the Pacific, several less-than-reliable attempts have been made to claim that the dispersed island chains are the remnants of the once-great (but entirely fictional) continent and civilisation of Mu. And the imaginary land of Hy-Brasil, which features extensively in Irish legend as a magical, mystical realm off the west coast of Ireland, was still being reported as a genuine landfall for sailors as late as the 1670s. Indeed, the small rock of O'Brasil remained on nautical charts until 1850, when it was expunged on the reasonable grounds that it was entirely fictional.

THE MOVING COFFINS OF BARBADOS

In late 1812, members of the Chase family opened the door of their burial vault in Christchurch, Barbados. What they saw astonished them. The coffins containing the remains of two daughters of the family had been moved, with one actually standing on end. The coffins, which had been respectively deposited in the tomb in 1808 and in early 1812, were heavy, solid affairs and it would have required considerable force to disturb them. The vault was partly cut out of solid rock, with a heavy, locked door: there was no obvious means for a mischievous interloper to gain entry.

The episode remained just a peculiar one-off anomaly until the vault was opened to admit further burials on two occasions in 1816 and once in 1819 – for each time it was found that one or more coffins had been moved. The family determined to get to the bottom of the mystery, so they had the floor covered with sand to detect footprints, and ensured the door was fully secured.

By now the moving coffins were a sensation on the Caribbean island; so when the vault was scheduled to be opened again on 18 April 1820, a large crowd, including the colonial Governor, turned out to watch. The intact seals at the entrance were broken open, the door was swung back – and, once again, the witnesses were met with the sight of the coffins rearranged chaotically. Yet, bizarrely, there were no footprints in the sand. After this shock, the family had the coffins of their loved ones removed and buried elsewhere – and they remained undisturbed thereafter.

No convincing explanation has ever been put forward for the bizarre episode. Over the years various notions have suggested natural causes such as lightning strikes, earth tremors, vegetation growth, tidal movements and electromagnetic anomalies. Although intriguing and even ingenious, none of these ideas have moved from the realm of speculation into testable hypotheses. On the supernatural front, the disturbances have been put down to everything from telekinesis to poltergeist activity. Interestingly, no-one seems to have suggested that the coffins were being moved by their inhabitants – the idea of the undead shuffling their wooden prisons around perhaps being not a very appealing one. An obvious possibility is that someone within, or associated with, the Chase family gained access to the tomb to perpetuate a hoax – but, once again, this idea founders on the lack of evidence. Ultimately, the mystery of the 'Moving Coffins of Barbados' remains unsolved.

THE MYSTERY OF KASPER HAUSER

The tale of Kasper Hauser is an enduring mystery, a classic case that continues to fascinate and baffle researchers to this day.

In May 1828 a peculiarly dressed young man with a strange air about him was found wandering about the marketplace of the German city of Nuremberg. Despite being apparently the height and size of a 16-year-old, he had almost no social skills, spoke German as if he was a small child, and was carrying two enigmatic letters. One letter was supposedly penned by his mother, stating that the youth was the illegitimate son of a cavalry officer; as she was too poor to raise her little Kasper, as she named him, she had deposited the infant with a caring peasant family. The second letter was purportedly written by this adoptive family, requesting that Kasper be enrolled in a cavalry regiment so that he could follow in his father's footsteps. These letters raised many unanswered questions, not least how it was that both a poor unmarried mother and a peasant family possessed the necessary literary skills to put pen to paper. In addition, Kasper's 'otherworldly' quality meant he was unfit for any kind of work, never mind a military career. It was suggested that the letters were forgeries or hoaxes, but if they were, who had written them, and for what purpose?

The mystery deepened when Kasper talked about his upbringing, saying he had been kept in a hole in the ground, isolated from all human contact apart from a 'carer' who provided the minimum of his needs. He did not know this man's name, but identified him as the person who had abandoned him in the marketplace. Kasper's poorly developed mental, linguistic and emotional faculties were consistent with him having been denied meaningful social interaction, and in some ways he resembled the 'feral children' who were supposed to have been abandoned by their parents and partly raised by animals.

For this reason, Kasper attracted the attention of scientists who were interested in studying what we now call developmental psychology, or the processes that turn us from dependent infants into fully functioning adults. Kasper received care and education. His social and language skills improved gradually, but he was forever to be a 'child of nature' rather than a member of human society. Those who studied him claimed his senses of smell and sight were much more acute than those in an average human, a situation put down to his body adapting to the almost lightless environment in which he was raised.

Inevitably, Kasper's strange story – prompted by his growing fame – launched a series of speculations. Why, it was asked, would someone want to confine this otherwise unremarkable youth in a dark hole in the ground, and go to the expense of feeding and caring for him over many years? The obvious conclusion was that he was someone important – a minor but crucial player in some dynastic intrigue. Eventually, the story went about that Kasper was the son of the powerful Karl, Grand Duke of Baden, who had died in 1818. It was suggested that the infant Kasper had been smuggled out of the Duke's palace and his place taken by a sickly substitute. When the fake child died, as was planned all along, the Duke had no heir, and so on his death the title passed to an uncle, presumed to be the unscrupulous progenitor of the scheme. Kasper should have been killed, but the conspirators did not have the heart to do the deed. Only when the child became a difficult-to-handle strapping youth did the 'caretaker' release the boy into the world.

So ran the conspiracy theory, and indeed DNA tests on Kasper's coat – which still exists in Nuremberg – suggests the boy was possibly related to the royal family of Baden. On the other hand, many people at the time suggested that Kasper was an imposter. Certainly parts of his story did not stack up – he claimed, for example, to have consumed just bread and water throughout his imprisonment, but he was well nourished, and so clearly had had access to a protein-rich diet.

If Kasper's origins were a mystery, the rest of his short life continued to ramp up the bizarre quotient. A year after he was 'discovered', he claimed to have been attacked by a hooded man wielding a knife. For some observers it was proof positive that powerful vested interests were seeking to eliminate the inconvenient youth. For others, the wound was self-inflicted, a sign of the imposter's desperate attempt to bolster his story. Then on 14 December 1833 a man wearing a black cloak stabbed Kasper, the wound proving fatal three days later. Even at the time, some accused him of having attempted to commit suicide, a charge he strongly denied.

Kasper Hauser was on the world stage for just five years, during which his story divided scientists, educated observers and the great and the good. To this day, he remains an enigma. His story has prompted speculation that he was a visitor from another dimension, or a time traveller; that he was a simpleton simply abandoned by his carers; or that he was a devious, self-serving hoaxster. Even after all this time, we still do not know what really happened to that otherworldly youth who appeared in the busy marketplace of a German city in 1828.

VISIONS OF THE VIRGIN MARY

Mary, the mother of Jesus, conceived her son through divine intervention (or 'without sin' as the official euphemism has it), and in the Middle Ages she became a major cult figure within the Roman Catholic church, often providing a devotional focus for female worshippers. She remains the most significant Catholic figure outside Jesus and God the Father, and is often referred to as the Madonna or the Blessed Virgin Mary (BVM).

'Marian apparitions', as they are known in the literature, are widely reported from both the period when all of Europe was Catholic, and from Roman Catholic communities worldwide today. The basic phenomenon is the appearance of a mystical female spirit, usually clothed in the conventional attire of the BVM as shown in religious paintings. She often speaks to the visionary, exhorting an increase in, or return to, religious faith, and sometimes she offers prophecies or dire warnings for the future.

There are numerous Marian apparitions and visions from the historical period, the first dating to AD 40 when she appeared to St James the Apostle. 'Our Lady of Guadeloupe' was seen by a Mexican peasant in 1531. María de Agreda, a 17th-century Spanish nun and mystic, wrote a book entitled *The Mystical City of God* based on the revelations she received from the Virgin Mary (María was supposedly also able to 'bilocate' or teleport, as she preached in New Mexico and Texas without ever leaving Spain). Closer to home, and a century earlier, Bishop Gavin Dunbar of Aberdeen was instructed by the Virgin Mary to build a bridge over the River Dee.

In more recent times, visions of the BVM have been the focus of extraordinary outpourings of devotion, faith, and religious infrastructure. The famous French pilgrimage site of Lourdes, which attracts millions of visitors a year, owes its origin to the Marian visions of a single 14-year-old girl in 1858. The Catholic Church has officially recognised more than 60 miracles of healing at Lourdes. The village of Knock, in County Mayo in the Republic of Ireland, is now a major international destination (it even has its own airport) because 15 people had a shared vision of the Madonna in 1879. The small Portuguese village of Fátima is the third major European Marian pilgrimage site, and is possibly the most extraordinary. In 1917 three peasant children had a series of repeated visions of the Virgin Mary, in which the divine mother urged the world to repent, and to worship herself as the route to God. After the apparitions ceased huge crowds gathered at the spot and in September 1917 some kind of mass phenomenon took place, with many people saying they had seen the sun 'dance' in the sky (although others in the crowd experienced nothing unusual). This much-debated event may have been a case of mass hysteria brought about by religious expectation, but no-one knows for certain. Even stranger, the Virgin had entrusted the children with hidden knowledge or prophecies, known as 'the Three Secrets of Fátima'. The first was a description of the torments of Hell that awaited unrepentant sinners. The second told of a second global war that would consume the world unless humankind returned to the paths of God (remember this was in 1917, during what was then known as the Great War – the conflict we call the *First* World War). The third Secret was kept hidden by the Vatican and only revealed in the year 2000. It described a bishop dressed in white dying in a hail of bullets. According to the Vatican, the vision was a prediction of the assassination attempt on the Pope in Rome in 1981, and John Paul II himself ascribed his survival to the divine intervention of the Virgin. One of the bullets used by the gunman now sits in the crown of the Madonna's statue at Fátima.

In contrast to these officially recognised places of Marian devotion, other more recent locations are more controversial. The immensely popular site of Medjugorje in Herzegovina in the former Yugoslavia has never been approved by the Catholic Church as 'worthy of belief', and the collective Marian apparition allegedly seen there by six local youths in 1981 remains a subject of great debate. Another popular manifestation at San Sebastian de Garabandal in Spain, dating from

1961, has not received the Vatican's official imprimatur, which is also the case with the Marian apparitions reported from New York State between 1970 and 1995.

Visions and apparitions of the BVM continue to be occasionally noted in the media. For the faithful they are acts of divine favour and guidance, while to some non-Catholics they seem explicable only in terms of cultural, psychological or social needs – and it has not gone unnoticed that many Marian visitations coincide with times of war, economic distress, or other social ills.

MOVING, WEEPING AND BLEEDING STATUES

In 1985, a group of worshippers at the Irish open-air Marian shrine at Ballinspittal claimed they saw the statue of the Virgin Mary move. The news flashed around the world and soon similar reports were generated from dozens of Marian sites from many different countries. Between 1919 and 1922 several towns in Spain generated reports of the image of Christ writhing in agony on the Cross, or of saints stepping down from the church walls to move around. In 1973 a Japanese Catholic nun, Sister Agnes Sasagawa, had a religious ecstatic experience, which centred on blood flowing from 'wounds' on a wooden statuette of the Virgin Mary; the 'blood' later became a clear liquid more akin to tears or sweat. In 1995, a statue of the Virgin Mary bought at the Balkan Marian apparition site at Medjugorje was installed in the Italian port of Civitavechia, and promptly started to 'weep' tears of blood.

Weeping icons of the Virgin Mary have been reported from Eastern Europe since at least the 1600s, while similar weeping or bleeding images are known from Italy, the very heart of Catholic belief, from 1485. But it is only since the 1970s that these few isolated examples have become a veritable flood of Marian images and statues that bleed and cry. Examples can be found from around 25 countries and across every continent – one European example is the famous 'weeping Madonna' at Maasmechelen in Belgium. As with the Marian apparitions discussed above, these supposedly miraculous statues quickly attract local cults (and sometimes national and international followings). Although the Virgin Mary is the focus of the majority of the phenomena, images of her son are also miraculously aqueous. In 1911, a painting in Mirebeau, France, bled from the palms and forehead (the traditional location of the stigmata or wounds Christ received during the Crucifixion). And in 1996 a fresco of Jesus in the Church of the Nativity in Bethlehem began to weep bloody tears. Other cases of sanguinary statues of Jesus have been reported from Sicily, Brazil, Ireland and Pennsylvania.

In several cases, scientists have shown the liquids to be outright hoaxes, as with the case of a statue of the Virgin Mary in the Australian city of Brisbane in 2002, where analysis demonstrated that the 'holy oil' the image was exuding was in fact a commercial product introduced through a pair of deliberately drilled holes. It is probable that some other 'divine bodily fluids' are similar pious frauds. Sceptics would say that bleeding and weeping statues are more common than moving ones because liquids are relatively easy to fake, while making statues move in an apparent supernatural manner is logistically challenging. In other cases, it has been difficult to come to a definitive conclusion – investigation of the still-controversial Civitavechia case, for example, has been stalled because although the red liquid flowing from the Virgin Mary's tear ducts has been shown to be *male* human blood, the family involved have refused to submit to DNA tests. On the other hand, the Japanese case mentioned above has been judged by the Catholic Church to be 'reliable and worthy of belief'. The approval was granted in 1988 by the Congregation for the Doctrine of the Faith, the body that used to be called the Inquisition and is now charged with investigating alleged divine events. The head of the Congregation at the time was Cardinal Ratzinger, who is now Pope Benedict XVI.

The relationship between holy images and divine liquids is not however confined to Christianity. In Kerala, India, the statue of the Hindu goddess Bhagawati (Parvati) is believed to menstruate. And, over three days in September 1995, Hindu communities around the world were reporting that statues of the elephant-headed god Ganesh were regularly 'drinking' offerings of milk.

SPONTANEOUS HUMAN COMBUSTION

It takes temperatures of several hundred degrees centigrade to reduce a human body to ash, and even then typically some bones remain. Our skeletons, it turns out, are astonishingly tough, and crematoria have to use a machine to crush into powder the bones that remain after being subject to burning that can be as high as 950°C. The human body in general does not burn easily because so much of it is composed of water. At first glance, all this would suggest that spontaneous human combustion is impossible. SHC, as it is commonly abbreviated, is supposed to be the partial or total consumption of a human body by fire, without any obvious cause. In a typical SHC case, bones are reduced to ash, but nearby flammable objects, such as wooden furniture, remain unharmed. If the fire had reached a *minimum* of 600°C, as required by the standard physics of human burning, then all these objects should have gone up in flames. Yet, despite these objections, a small number of scientists and fire investigators contend that SHC is a genuine phenomenon.

A classic case of SHC was reported from Aberdeen in 1888. Unlike most cases before the 20th century, it was not only investigated by a professional doctor, but the corpse was also photographed. Dr. J. Mackenzie Booth, Physician to the Aberdeen General Dispensary and Lecturer on 'Diseases of the Ear and Larynx' at the University of Aberdeen, wrote a detailed account of the case for the *British Medical Journal*. He described how the 'old soldier' had fallen asleep in a loft, and twelve hours later was found burned to a cinder. The prone body had retained its shape, but when it was picked up the entire corpse, including all the large bones, crumbled to powder. Yet the loft was filled with lumber and hay, none of which had caught fire.

Perhaps the most famous SHC case is that of Mary Reeser, who perished in Florida in 1951. The episode was thoroughly investigated by the authorities because the only part of Mrs Reeser's body that remained in her apartment was her left foot, complete with its black satin slipper. Despite the almost total burning of a twelve-stone woman, most of the wooden objects in the room were untouched. And in their book *Spontaneous Human Combustion*, authors Jenny Randles and Peter Hough investigated several similar contemporary cases from West Yorkshire, London and the Midlands – cases that had been reviewed by senior fire experts, who were convinced abnormal fires were involved.

Although there are apparent accounts of SHC from the ancient world, it is not until 1725 that we come across a case that is half reliable in its account. Nicole Millet's husband was accused of her murder when she was found completely burned in Rheims, France. He was acquitted when the court found that the fire was not the result of human action, but by 'a visitation from God'. SHC was back in the courtroom in 1850, when John Stauff was accused of the murder of the Countess Goerlitz in Darmstadt, Germany. The defence suggested the Countess's fiery death was due to SHC, an argument several physicians – and the court – rejected, and Stauff was imprisoned for life. The fact that SHC was seriously considered shows how well known the idea was in the 19th century. In part this was due to the widely read Italian case of the Countess Cornelia Bandi of Cesena, who, according to the official report, died in 1745 from fire kindled ...

> 'in the entrails by the inflamed effluvia of the blood, by the juices and fermentation in the stomach, and, lastly, by fiery evaporations which exhaled from the spirits of wine, brandy, etc.'

Overindulgence in alcohol was a common theory for SHC in the 1700s and 1800s, but this has since been shown to be a smokescreen, as the combustion of human tissue is unaffected by whether it contains no alcohol at all, or is saturated in the stuff. On the other hand, if victims are insensible due to drinking, this may explain why they do not wake up when they start burning. Another notion is the 'wick effect', in which an external heat source such as a cigarette or oil-burning lamp starts a slow-burning fire in the victim's clothes, and the combustion is kept going for a long time by 'wicking' up fats from the body. All attempts to replicate this process have ended in failure, as insufficient heat is generated to create the temperatures required to reduce a human body to ash.

One clue as to the nature of SHC may be found in a variety of strange accounts between 1750 and 1850 (always assuming they are accurate, of course). Two butchers reported flames coming out of animals they were cutting up, and several doctors described fire apparently erupting from their patients' mouths, backsides and private parts, with one account describing a small flame appearing during the process of giving birth. It remains an outside possibility that some currently unknown physiological process within the human body may on rare occasions spontaneously produce fire – but so far there is not a shred of scientific evidence for this.

Not surprisingly SHC has attracted the attentions of creative writers. It first appears in the Gothic novel *Wieland*, published in 1796 by Charles Brockden Brown. Later appearances can be found in works by notable writers such as Captain Frederick Marryat,

Nikolai Gogol, Herman Melville, Mark Twain, Emile Zola and Thomas de Quincey. The most famous literary SHC case is from Charles Dickens' 1852 novel *Bleak House*, in which the fate is visited upon the drunken rag-and-bottle merchant, Krook. *Bleak House* may have done more than anything else to bring SHC into public consciousness, not least because it sparked a public debate between believers and sceptics. One of SHC's more recent media appearances has been in the US television series *CSI* (*Crime Scene Investigation*). The series' chief investigator, Gus Grissom, sets up an experiment with a dead pig and a slow-burning fire, and 'proves' that SHC does not exist. In the real world the debate remains unresolved.

BALL LIGHTNING

This term refers to moving and glowing balls of light that have usually been witnessed during thunderstorms. The short-lived phenomenon of ball lightning has never been fully explained, with common notions invoking plasma fields (a state of matter in which ionized particles can conduct high-energy electromagnetic forces), radiation or microwave energy. All that is really known is that the floating balls appear to be attracted to metal objects, and also often move towards humans (perhaps because our nervous system is partly electromagnetic in nature). Sometimes people are burned by contact with the ball, or thrown a distance of several feet, as with more usual lightning strikes. On other occasions the 'ball' passes without any ill effects. Ball lightning (whatever it is) has been observed to move through walls into buildings, and even on one occasion roll down the aisle of a passenger aircraft during a thunderstorm.

Because no-one knows what ball lightning really is it can sometimes be used as a catch-all for a variety of unexplained phenomena. Crop circles, corpse or death lights, Will-o'-the-wisps, and sightings of UFOs, fairies and some 'amorphous' ghosts, have all been plausibly linked with ball lightning, but there is no conclusive proof. Certainly we still have a great deal to learn about our weather and electromagnetism. It was only in 2008, for example, that we discovered 'elves' and 'sprites' – bursts of lightning shaped like jellyfish and doughnuts respectively that erupt in the upper atmosphere *above* thunderstorms. Several claims have been made that ball lightning has been recreated in a laboratory, although other scientists remain unconvinced. We can but hope that as our understanding of the wonders of the natural world continues to increase, we will one day 'bottle' ball lightning.

EARTHLIGHTS

A phenomenon that may or may not be connected to ball lightning has been dubbed 'earthlights' by researcher Paul Devereux. These are strange lights seen in the landscape that may be caused by electromagnetic anomalies created by geological faulting. In 1919 a Mr. T. Sington and a companion saw several such strange lights moving back and forth at Castlerigg in the Lake District, now one of the most visited stone circles in the country. As they were watching from behind a boundary wall, one of the lights came straight towards them.

'When it came close to the wall it slowed down, stopped, quivered and slowly went out,' wrote Mr Sington later, 'as if the matter producing the light had become exhausted. It was globular, white, with a nucleus, possibly 6 feet or so in diameter, and just high enough above the ground to pass over our heads.'

Several similar encounters have been reported at other stone circles from around the country, such as the Merry Maidens in Cornwall and Stanton Drew in Somerset. It has been theorised that the earthlights may have been seen at these places for millennia, thus providing the impetus to build circles at the 'abode of the gods'. Similarly, earthlights may provide an explanation for some close encounters with fairies, UFOs, and other supposedly paranormal visitors. And if earthlights are electromagnetic in nature, they may interfere with our nervous systems, thus potentially creating hallucinations and anomalous experiences. As with ball lightning, there is the danger of using one currently unexplained phenomenon – earthlights – to 'explain' other unexplained phenomena. However, the earthlights idea may be one that deserves some serious scientific analysis.

Chapter 2

PARAPSYCHOLOGY

Parapsychology is the study of mysterious powers of the mind. Although often linked to the world of spirits and ghosts – and indeed there is frequently overlap between the various fields – here we will confine it to mental phenomena such as telepathy, psychokinesis, and claims that humans can see into the future or perform feats of healing.

What parapsychologists study is sometimes called Extra-Sensory Perception (ESP) – meaning the ability of some people to get information about their environment without the use of normal sensory channels. ESP as a term has largely fallen out of favour, and the preferred current term is 'psi'.

TELEPATHY

Although commonly regarded as 'mind reading', telepathy seems to be a much more complex and subtle affair. The term was coined in 1882 and from its Greek roots literally means 'distant feeling'. It is used to describe information being passed from one living person to another without any form of normal sensory communication. In many cases telepathic communication is reported over a distance, so that the two individuals are not even in visual contact.

One of the curiosities that parapsychologists have found is that telepathic communication does not involve much in the way of language or words being transmitted – instead the percipient appears to receive images. This has led to a number of experiments where a 'sender' attempts to mentally transmit a visual image they are looking at (such as a shape, drawing or a film clip) to a 'receiver'. Although such experiments sometimes show a slight statistical result that seems to favour a paranormal explanation, telepathy, and psi in general, are notoriously difficult to demonstrate in the laboratory.

A reason why this is the case may come from analysis of what are termed 'spontaneous' cases, where individuals out of the blue receive information that they then act upon. The most typical spontaneous cases involve two people who are emotionally close – for example, a mother has a sentiment that her child is in danger, decides to drive to the school, and finds that an accident has just occurred. Or someone suddenly 'knows' that a sibling, partner or parent has been injured, makes a call, and finds that, indeed, the individual is in a bad way. What all these spontaneous cases have in common is that the information communicated is *urgent* – a message of *crisis* delivered not through words but via *images*. In the laboratory, there is no crisis, and hence the mechanism of telepathy is rarely engaged there.

The reaction in these spontaneous cases is an emotional one, and a case is being made by some researchers that telepathy functions by utilising, not the mind, but the body's emotional system. Psi researcher, Richard Bradley, in a 2006 paper for *The Journal of Parapsychology*, has argued that this entire process has been evolved over thousands of years, and that it gives us an evolutionary advantage. In other words, most of the time our five senses – sight, hearing, touch, smell and taste – are perfectly adequate to cope with ordinary events. But when a crisis erupts – a threat to ourselves or to our loved ones – then telepathic information is communicated via a 'sixth sense' or 'extrasensory perception'. The information is directed to our emotional system, which is not under conscious control, and is also responsible for our 'flight-or-fight' response, which is what kicks in during a crisis or a threat. The flight-or-fight system fires urgent images into the conscious mind, and we instantly react to the threat on an emotional rather than a rational level. In this analysis, telepathy is the 'emergency channel', and so only comes into play during times of danger.

Recent research also seems to show that this emergency channel is more likely to work when there is both an emotional and a genetic bond between the two participants. Typically this means parent-child or sibling–sibling, but there is a strong suggestion that the strongest bond is between twins. There is one case on record of a teacher collapsing with chest pains in front of his class – but then he recovered, and an examination showed that he had not suffered any heart problems. But his twin brother, who lived some distance away, had suffered a serious heart attack at the same moment. In this case the 'telepathy' did not involve the transmission of words or even images – just the sensation of massive pain.

If telepathy is real, it may underlie other areas of the paranormal. One of the most commonly reported types of ghost is what is called a 'crisis apparition'. This is where an individual appears to someone they love, even though they are a great distance away. Often the apparition speaks as well as moves, or sometimes just the voice is heard. The apparition typically appears to be in distress, or wishes to convey a message or to say goodbye. It is then found that the person died shortly after the time of the appearance. It is possible that the apparition was not a spirit, but a telepathic communication from the mind of the dying individual. Even stranger, telepathy provides a plausible means for the knowledge acquired by genuine mediums – perhaps they are not picking up messages from the dead, but instead unconsciously 'scanning' their clients by the telepathic channel.

None of this, of course, explains just how the information is transmitted. The mechanism for telepathy has not just remained unfound – we do not even know where to look. The evolutionary suggestion also does not account for the fact that reports of spontaneous cases of emotional telepathy are actually very rare – although hundreds of cases have been collected, most people in a crisis do not have such experiences.

Telepathy, then, is a curiosity in paranormal research. We have a small number of cases which seem to demonstrate an objective reality for a communication process that does not involve the known senses. These cases seem to suggest the process only activates during a crisis, and is hard, if not impossible, to recreate under supervised conditions. We have qualified researchers who are convinced the communication is genuine. But we have no evidence whatsoever for the mechanism of this transmission.

PRECOGNITION

In 1951, a 25-year-old man burst into tears when he learnt that his brother-in-law, Bob, was about to drive to San Jose, in California. He begged him not to go, creating a scene which delayed the departure by 15 minutes, during which time Bob's co-driver became impatient and left. Bob therefore had no choice but to use his own car. What happened next was reported in L. E. Rhine's book *Hidden Channels of the Mind*:

> '[Bob] got as far as Bayshore and Charter streets, when the traffic began to back up. A wreck, which is nothing unusual around here, but when Bob got to the corner, he said he almost passed out. There spread out on the highway was the man he was to have ridden with; his head was half gone. The car was a total loss. They found later that his brakes had locked on one side, and he flipped up in the air and came down on the other side of the road to be hit head-on by another car.'

This case is typical of hundreds of reports of precognition, or receiving information of future events via extrasensory means. In many ways precognition appears to function in a similar way to telepathy, in that it usually communicates danger or crisis via emotions and images. And like telepathy, it is frustratingly elusive for scientific researchers. There is also the added difficulty that the mechanism appears to operate not only across distance but across time itself. And the information from the future may come while the person is fully awake or during dreams, and may relate to just the next few minutes or to some time days or weeks in the future.

There is no way of telling how many people have mild precognitive experiences that they do not even notice – they simply have a feeling or a 'hunch', and do X instead of Y. If they had chosen Y, it is possible something awful would have happened – but we will never know. It is also difficult to sift real precognitive events from the mass of expectations, fears, projections, plans, daydreams and fantasies that make up the daily internal mental processes of most of us. If I see an image of a car crash in my mind, and an accident later takes place the same day, was that precognition or simply me being worried about driving on a notoriously dangerous road? And in many cases precognition is only noticed *after* the event, and so we may construct a narrative that brings the mental image and the event together, even though it may just be a coincidence – but it makes for an interesting story to tell to your friends, doesn't it?

It is easier to pinpoint cases where the precognitive episode has prompted a change in behaviour, such as in the Californian incident cited above. In these cases the individual clearly reacts in a way that *alters* the projected future, so that danger is avoided. It is thus clearly adaptive, that is, it has an evolutionary advantage (because the percipient or those emotionally close to the percipient do not die, and survive). It is therefore possible that, like telepathy, precognition kicks in during an emergency, and is something we have adapted to over millennia.

But how can precognition possibly work? Surely the future is unknowable, because by definition it has not happened yet? Well here we enter the truly weird world of high-energy subatomic particle research. Cutting-edge physics involving the analysis of infinitesimally brief quantum events has suggested that the apparently impossible is actually all too probable. Multiple parallel universes may be 'peeling off' our own at key events (when X happens instead of Y); the future may 'exist' as a cloud of probabilities before it happens; and information may be exchanged between the future and the present.

This bizarre set of counter-intuitive notions, which goes against everything we regard as 'normal', is now becoming mainstream opinion in advanced institutions. As yet we are on the baby slopes of this brave new world of weird science, and we do not know where this new research will take us. Possibly, just possibly, one application will be an investigation of precognition.

PSYCHOKINESIS (PK)

In the early 1970s, a young Israeli named Uri Geller appeared in British television and proceeded to bend spoons apparently using only the power of his mind. It was an utter sensation, one of the key moments in the recent history of the paranormal. Some older readers may remember attending 'spoon-bending' parties at the time, sitting around in a circle and speaking or shouting at cutlery in the hope that they could imitate 'that man off the telly'. Geller remains the most famous self-proclaimed psychic practitioner in the world, and owns a Cadillac decorated with more than 5,000 examples of bent cutlery.

Psychokinesis or PK literally means 'movement by the mind'. Geller may have introduced the word to the wider world, but the topic has been around for many years for its obvious interest and applicability. During the Victorian period, in opposition to the spiritualist insistence on the reality of the spirits of the dead, it was suggested as an alternative explanatory mechanism for the levitations occurring at séances. In the 1960s, the Soviet military investigated Nina Kulagina, who was said to be able to mentally move small objects and even control the beating of a frog's dissected heart. More recently, as documented in Jon Ronson's book *The Men Who Stare at Goats*, the US military attempted (without success) to train soldiers to stop a goat's heart using just the power of their minds.

In theory, psychokinesis should be one of the easiest of all the parapsychological powers to test – after all, either an object moves or it does not. In practice, however, PK is just as slippery as its fellows. Nina Kulagina and Uri Geller both remain highly controversial, while laboratory tests have not produced conclusive results, and stage magicians claim to have imitated metal bending feats using the illusions and tricks of their craft. Parapsychologists have thus divided their field of investigation into two subjects, called Macro-PK and Micro-PK. Macro-PK covers effects that are visible to the naked eye such as the obvious movement of an object (or the bending of a spoon). Micro-PK involves mental effects that cannot be detected by sight, typically a laboratory test to influence the numbers produced by a device called a

Random Number Generator or RNG. The RNG does what it says, randomly selecting long lines of numbers that cannot be predicted. The purpose of Micro-PK tests is to attempt to make the RNG produce desired numbers, thus showing that PK can influence events at the electronic level. Success in RNG experiments would only be found in the analysis of large numbers of statistics, which is not particularly glamorous or newsworthy. But even if results of statistical significance were found, it could be countered that the operatives were demonstrating precognition, not psychokinesis. As it happens, neither Macro-PK nor Micro-PK experiments have produced anything of indisputable value.

So is psychokinesis something that we should take seriously? Can the human mind project an (unknown) force in an (unknown) manner via an (unknown) mechanism to actually influence the world of matter? Bizarrely enough, the answer may possibly come from a subject most people associate with the world of ghosts, not the realm of parapsychology – poltergeists.

POLTERGEISTS

In the early 1970s, American parapsychologist, William G. Roll, analysed 116 poltergeist cases from around the world, including a small number that he or a colleague had personally investigated. His pioneering research, based on ideas initially put forward by psychologist, Nandor Fodor, in the 1930s, accelerated the move away from treating poltergeists as ghosts or hauntings, and towards the idea that they were in fact examples of parapsychological phenomena. This approach, seeing 'polts' not as spirit-based but mind-based, is one that is followed by the majority of researchers today.

Polter and *geist* are respectively the German words for 'noisy' and 'spirit'. The verb *poltern* means to make knocking or rumbling sounds, or to create a racket. The word 'poltergeist' was first used by German researchers and was introduced into the English language in 1848 by the writer Catherine Crowe, in her classic and still-relevant book, *The Night-Side of Nature*. Poltergeists are easily among the most demonstrative of paranormal phenomena. Typical manifestations include:

- The movement of objects, including throwing, dropping, smashing and overturning everything from small cups to large pieces of furniture. Sometimes objects are thrown at a specific target.

- Objects 'disappearing' and returning at a later date, either to the original location or to another place.

- Objects being displaced 'through' walls so that they appear as if out of nowhere – in other words, teleportation. If these objects have been brought from somewhere beyond the house, they are known as 'apports'.

- The levitation of objects or people. Bedclothes are a favourite.

- Spontaneous floods or fires. Sometimes the fires go out of their own accord.

- Foul smells, or the introduction of blood, oil and other more noxious substances into places where they do not belong.

- Interference with telephones and electrical items. Brand new batteries drain, recently checked equipment malfunctions, televisions or music players spontaneously turn on or off, lights flicker, bulbs blow, and phones ring with no-one on the line.

- Ridiculously high electricity bills without any corresponding electrical usage.

- Noises, from low raps and knocks to loud bangs, animal sounds and horrid voices.

- 'Rains' of stones, coins or other small objects; sometimes these rains fall on the roof of the house, but at other times they manifest indoors.

- Temperature variations, such as 'cold spots'.

- Messages, often malevolent or nonsensical. These can arrive via graffiti on walls, the rearranging of children's play letters, or over the telephone. In the South Shields case (see page 82) spoken messages were apparently delivered through toy figures.

- Pinching, scratching and tormenting people. Often the person who suffers the most is the poltergeist focus (see below).

- Apparitions (only very rarely).

Even before the word was known, poltergeists were widely reported. The first detailed description of a poltergeist incident came in 1612, from Mascon, France, the incidents taking place in the home of Francis Perrault, a Protestant minister. Perrault's account was published in English at the behest of the famous British scientist, Robert Boyle. Elsewhere in the 17th century we find cases from Maidenhead in Berkshire, Little Burton and South Cadbury in Somerset, and, in Wiltshire, the 'Drummer of Tedworth' (which manifested when a drum was confiscated). A very famous episode took place in a vicarage in the Lincolnshire village of Epworth in 1716–17, the victims being the family of the Reverend Samuel Wesley, including John Wesley, the founder of Methodism.

In 1817, the Bell Witch outbreak in Tennessee lasted for more than three years and attracted considerable notoriety, largely through the aggressive and malevolent nature of the phenomena. In 1903, falls of stones appeared in a bedroom in Sumatra, even though there was no route in through the roof – and the stones *changed their direction in the air* to prevent their being caught before hitting the floor. In every case, these and other similar manifestations were blamed on spirits, witches/sorcerers, or the Devil.

Roll's idea was that the poltergeist was actually attached to a living person, an individual known as the 'poltergeist focus' or simply the 'focus'. The focus almost always lived in the household suffering the attacks, and in the majority of cases was under the age of twenty-one. Roll suggested that the inner turmoil of the focus (such as the onset of puberty, or frustration with a family situation) unconsciously manifested as physical phenomena. In this view, the poltergeist is a form of psychokinesis. The repetitive but irregular nature of the phenomena caused Roll to use the term 'Recurrent Spontaneous Psychokinesis' or RSPK. RSPK in poltergeist cases may now provide more evidence for psychokinesis than laboratory experiments.

Roll found that the average duration for a polt outbreak was between two and five months, after which the events rarely if ever reoccured. Sometimes the phenomena followed if the focus moved elsewhere, or even if the person went out of the house for a short time. In many cases things started relatively quietly, with a few strange noises, and only escalated to full-blown chaos over time. In a number of cases the 'polt' became responsive, as if it had intelligence, responding to people knocking by giving the same number of raps, and even appearing to answer simple questions. In the 1612 French case an investigator found the polt would echo his whistles, tone for tone and duration for duration (it also flung back stones that had been marked for identification and thrown 'towards' it). Often the presence of an investigator, especially a sceptical or scientifically minded one, served to 'stir up' the poltergeist, as if it was keen to prove its own existence.

In 1976, William Roll also analysed what was known about the focal persons. More than half had medical conditions, ranging from epilepsy and seizures to a variety of severe organic ailments such as tuberculosis and kidney disease, or a host of psychological problems including anxiety attacks, disturbed sleep, sleepwalking, hyperactivity, fugue states and extreme irritation. Many of the focal children had recently undergone a disturbing experience, such as their parents' divorce or other family breakdown, a bereavement or funeral, a financial downturn, illness or a move to a new house. A majority of focal persons were female. And almost always, the events ceased when the focal person was asleep.

This led Roll to suggest that the typical poltergeist focus is a female between the age of 12 and 19, with a troubled emotional or family life, and a background of medical or psychological problems. But of course, as Roll himself admits, this is just the result of a statistical analysis, with an emphasis on averages and weighted numbers. There are plenty of poltergeist cases where the focus is male, with no apparent or significant problems or other deviations from the 'standard analysis'.

Roll's study is valuable in that it shows us what connects a small majority of cases; but it is far from being the full story. And a small number of poltergeist incidents have elements that overlap with hauntings, where the evidence suggests 'discarnate entities' (the preferred term rather than 'ghost' or 'spirit') may be present. Or possibly these cases are the outer extreme of the poltergeist experience, and the discarnate entities are themselves creations of the focus' unconscious ire and frustration.

Some poltergeist effects have been shown to have a verifiable, objective existence. In 1967–68, for example, electrical equipment was going haywire in a lawyer's office in Rosenheim, Germany (furniture and objects were also moved, along with other standard poltergeist activity, such as telephone calls appearing on the phone company's system when no calls had been made). A pair of physicists set up a recorder in the office to measure the electrical flow. Over an hour and a quarter the voltage in the office's cables showed anomalous peaks no less than 15 times, often accompanied by loud bangs. The scientists ruled out hoaxing, fluctuations from the power grid, and known physical forces, and concluded the events were caused by 'mechanical influence without apparent cause'. In this case the focus was a 19-year-old secretary.

The most famous British outbreak took place at a London council house in 1977–78. Investigated over 13 months by Maurice Grosse and Guy Lyon Playfair of the Society for Psychical Research, 'The Enfield Poltergeist' produced a full range of extraordinary phenomena, often witnessed by the investigators or police officers, and on occasion captured by photographers or BBC audio engineers. The dual focus appeared to be the two eldest girls, who were 11 and 12 years old. As well as the movements, noises, equipment malfunctions and spontaneous fires and floods, the events also included the appearance of apparitions and an apparent ghost called Bill who seemed take over the vocal apparatus of one of the girls, speaking for many hours. Although some of the incidents were shown to have been faked by the children, this was interpreted as them 'helping things along' when the 'spirits' weren't cooperating with visitors. Both the investigators remained convinced the vast majority of the huge welter of phenomena were genuine. More recently, investigators Mike Hallowell and Darren Ritson have provided a meticulously detailed account of a disturbingly aggressive poltergeist infestation in the northeast of England during 2006. The 'South Shields Poltergeist' case not only included the usual range of phenomena, it also extended them into the digital age, with threatening text messages sent from supposedly disconnected numbers.

If RSPK exists, and is the real source for many poltergeist outbreaks, what could it be? One suggestion is that it is a form of energy, an energy that is as yet unidentified but still conforms to the known laws of the universe. The suggestion comes from 1967, when Roll and J. G. Pratt investigated a poltergeist case which was unusual in that it was concentrated not on a home but on a workplace. Employees and police officers had noticed a number of disturbances in a warehouse in Miami. Boxes of merchandise, plus individual glasses, beer mugs and ashtrays, were moving on the product shelves. During the study the pair of scientists observed that ten objects had moved or been smashed, and were able to measure the 'start point' and 'end point' of the movements. The focus was a 19-year-old shipping clerk named Julio, who was also under observation at the time, and hence could not have touched the objects. The investigators plotted the positions of the moved objects in relation to where Julio was standing, and marked the orientation of the objects that had been displaced. Spatial analysis suggested Julio's RSPK had operated in two 'waves' from his body, and that as he moved the 'waves' crossed, these crossing points causing the strongest movements. It also seemed that lighter objects travelled further than heavier ones, and the number of disturbed objects decreased the further the distance from the focal person – both of which are common properties of known energy sources.

As with telepathy and precognition, neither the mechanism nor the medium for RSPK have been identified. As to what could be the actual source of RSPK, the best guess at the moment is that it is caused by unusual neural discharges within the central nervous system. It may be no coincidence that a number of focal persons have suffered from seizures, epilepsy and repeated dissociative states, all of which are clinically associated with exceptional neural activity. On the other hand, not every focus exhibits these symptoms.

If RSPK is real, it will be identified through scientific research into the physics and chemistry of our brains and nerves, but it is early days yet.

The 'God Helmet'

One hint where this research may take us can be found in the work of Canadian neuroscientist, Michael Persinger. Persinger's interest lies in the temporal lobes of the brain, which, among other things, deal with our emotional experiences, our sense of 'who we are' (including memory) and 'where we are' in space and time, and how we understand language and the information perceived by our eyes, ears and nose. Persinger reasoned that disruptions in the temporal lobes might create distorted experiences which we wrongly interpret as 'paranormal'; he also considered that the temporal lobes might be the area where genuine psi information is transmitted through extra-low frequency electromagnetic waves (known, rather delightfully, as ELFs).

In some people the temporal lobes are affected by minute and brief electrical discharges that are associated with temporal lobe epilepsy or TLE. In some ways this medical term is rather unfortunate, as most people think of *grand mal* seizures when they hear the word 'epilepsy'. Individuals with mild TLE, however, do not usually suffer fits, and as far as they and any observers are concerned, they are perfectly normal. A number of us may occasionally experience short bursts of TLE, but will demonstrate no signs of epilepsy or abnormal personality. TLE is often undetectable to anyone who does not have the experience (and the technology) to look for it. The brief TLE discharges, however, can temporarily disrupt the normal functions of the temporal lobes and create anomalous events in the mind: to the person who experiences them the events are real, even though they are merely the product of a short-term disruption of part of the brain. Even mild TLE can distort time and space, create voices and visual hallucinations, promote a sense of falling or floating (such as floating up to a UFO), and produce feelings such as being outside your body (as in OOBEs – see page 125). In other words, it is possible that temporal lobe epilepsy is the medical condition behind a host of paranormal experiences. Perhaps when people report seeing elves they are merely getting a dose of ELFs.

Or not. Just because TLE *can* do these things, does not mean that it is the *cause* in all cases. Most people who report paranormal experiences are not tested for TLE, so there is no direct correlation. But it's worth keeping in mind that what sometimes appears to be *out there* may in some cases be *in here*.

Persinger has also investigated how electromagnetic waves affect our perceptions. To test this he constructed what is popularly known as the 'God Helmet', a laboratory tool that fires low-level electromagnetic waves at precise parts of the brain. Test subjects wearing the helmet have variously reported: a 'sense of presence' in the room; figures seen in the corner of the eyes, which disappear when the head is moved; emotions such as anxiety, or the feeling of being watched; a feeling that someone invisible was touching them on the shoulder; a sensation of mystical dreaminess or being 'out of it'; and even being in the presence of a divine or powerful being. The overlap with everything from UFO sightings to encounters with ghosts and religious experiences is obvious. Persinger has cautiously suggested that some paranormal experiences may be entirely subjective and internal in nature, caused when the subject is accidentally exposed to certain kinds of electromagnetic field.

One follow-up to this research has come at Muncaster Castle in Cumbria. Long famous for its ghosts, a series of experiments have shown that the metal-framed bed in the 'haunted bedroom' is actually at the centre of a strong magnetic field. People lying on the bed are subject to an invisible but powerful electromagnetic field; it is no coincidence that they then sense figures and other apparitions, for these are hallucinations created by being immersed in the field.

THOUGHTOGRAPHY

The 19th century was the heyday for a breed of spiritualist who claimed to be able to spontaneously create images on photographic plates using only the power of the mind. Many of these Victorian 'psychographs' now have an endearingly naive quality to them, and it takes an effort of will to imagine how they ever fooled anyone. Despite an initial surge of enthusiasm, thoughtography never really took off and, now that séances are no longer conducted in darkness, it has vanished from spiritualist practice.

In 1967, however, a strange man named Ted Serios brought 'thoughtography' into the living rooms of millions of television-watching Americans. Serios (1918–2006) would place a device he called his 'gizmo' over the lens of a Polaroid instant camera, stare manically through the tube, and transfer images from his mind onto the unexposed film. The resulting pictures were blurred and inconclusive, astonishing many but convincing few. If this was a kind of psychokinesis, it seemed spectacularly underwhelming. Sceptics contended that the gizmo – a kind of cardboard tube – contained some kind of optical device. Serios was uncooperative and frequently drunkenly aggressive, which made proper investigation difficult, but two amateur illusionists spotted him slipping something into the gizmo, and exposed him as a fraud in a photography magazine.

PSYCHIC SURGERY

In 21st-century Britain we are fortunate that we live in a period and country when proper medical treatment is widespread and available to all. But orthodox medicine cannot cure all ills, and pain, serious illness and disability often make people so desperate for alleviation or a cure that they will turn to the worlds of magic or parapsychology in the hope that this will relieve their suffering.

Paranormal healing in its broadest sense has been with us since the year dot, with practitioners variously called shamans, sorcerers, witch doctors, medicine men and traditional healers. During the period from the 15th century to the 18th century, much of the European witch craze was concerned with people who said they used magic for healing. Since the late 19th century, psychic healers have been claiming to balance the body's store of 'vital energy'. A host of New Age treatments such as Reiki, Therapeutic Touch and Aura Therapy have become popular in recent years. In modern times and in a Christian context we see practices such as faith healing, the laying on of hands, and pilgrimages to holy places where miraculous healing takes place such as Lourdes. Some of these healing activities are clearly religious in character and thus faith is said to be a necessary prerequisite. Other treatments are more secular in nature, and are available on the high street. In general anything that improves mental or emotional well-being can be said to be a good thing, and many patients report positive improvements to their physical health as well, although all responsible alternative therapists stress that their services only *complement* conventional medical treatment, and certainly do not replace it. If you are considering undergoing a form of alternative medicine, it is always a good idea to inform your GP. And be warned – some self-professed faith healers claim to be able to actually *cure* severe illnesses, such as cancer, and are happy to take your money for doing so. When stage magician and debunker James Randi investigated a number of US faith healers, two of the charlatans were sent to jail as a result. As ever, there are always unscrupulous characters around only too willing to exploit the needy and desperate.

But the most extreme – and controversial – form of paranormal healing is psychic surgery. Here the so-called 'surgeon' supposedly performs operations without anaesthetics or antiseptics, even without scalpels or other cutting tools. The psychic surgeon appears to delve directly into the patient's body with his fingers, and, after much blood has been produced, removes his hands, now holding the alleged cancerous growth, kidney stone or other damaged tissue. The 'incision' then seals itself without leaving a scar. The whole process is supposed to be possible because the surgeon has entered a paranormal 'vibrational state' which allows him to move through matter such as human flesh. Psychic surgeons are concentrated in the Philippines, Brazil, and Mexico, where they enjoy considerable success and incomes.

Observers of psychic surgery have noticed that a typical operation often has the air of a religious ritual. There are often many people present, with prayers being offered, invocation of deities (typically God, Jesus and the saints), chanting, call-and-response songs, even dancing and music. The surgeon himself is often creating a 'performance' through his ritualistic behaviour and 'mystic' hand movements. Each successful removal of diseased tissue may be greeted with more prayers and invocations. The whole process may create a sense of ecstasy, in which the participants are 'carried away' by the power of the ritual. But there is a problem – people who are in such a state of devotion and expectation are much easier to fool.

Not surprisingly, neither psychic surgeons nor their supporters welcome over-intrusive enquirers, but where it has been possible to examine the removed diseased tissue it has been shown to be nonhuman (for example, pieces of animal flesh or the livers of chickens and other fowls). In 1975 the Granada TV programme *World In Action* followed several British people who, despairing of orthodox medicine, travelled to the Philippines to consult psychic surgeons. As the programme showed, every single one of the British patients subsequently died, except for one who was merely rendered permanently blind. It was also shown how the surgeons, or *curanderos*, had an entire money-making infrastructure built around their psychic operations, from the hotels where the patients stayed, to restaurants and taxis.

James Randi and several other illusionists, such as Chris Angel and Penn and Teller, have studied the so-called miracles of psychic surgeons – and then reproduced them on stage or on television. Sleight-of-hand and distraction are employed, allowing the introduction of blood, fake incisions and removed tissue, all in a compelling and convincing manner – but all fake.

What of the patients who claim their dreadful illness has been cured? A comprehensive study is difficult because psychic surgeons do not operate like ordinary doctors – there is no follow-up, no assessment of the patient's recuperation, and no keeping of medical records. But several factors may be in play. The first is the well-known placebo effect, a psychological process whereby a patient recovers because they *believe* they have received effective treatment, even though they have been given a *placebo*, typically a sugared pill or foul-tasting liquid without any medical benefits. In the highly charged atmosphere of psychic surgery, it is easy to see how this process could operate. Anthropologists studying traditional medicine around the world have also found that a key element is the production of the 'bad thing' – the healer appears to pull out a thorn or pebble, and claims that this is the cause of the disease. The patient, seeing physical proof that his ailment is now outside his body, is satisfied, and is mentally prepared to heal. In psychic surgery, of course, the visibly produced 'bad thing' is the supposed cancerous tissue or kidney stone. Another likely factor is also psychological – a temporary remission of the pain, in which the believing patient walks away from the surgery in triumph and hope, only to succumb to the ravages of the disease when the enchantment wears off. And, once again, there is the tendency of the desperate and pain-ridden to believe almost anything.

Celebrities are just as prone to grasping at straws as the rest of us. Comedians Peter Sellers and Andy Kaufman both consulted Filipino *curanderos*. Both men were dreadfully ill (heart disease and cancer respectively), both handed over large sums of money, and both died shortly afterwards. Strangely enough, psychic surgeons do not offer refunds.

PSI, ILLUSION AND CHARLATANS

It is worth finishing this chapter with a general warning. Psi may be real; but that does not mean all apparent demonstrations of it are genuine. The British stage magician and television performer Derren Brown has replicated many of the activities associated with telepathy, precognition, telekinesis, mediumship, spiritualism, and a host of other psychic phenomena. Audience members are amazed that he seems to know their past, their relationships, even their thoughts. Objects move of their own accord. The future is accurately predicted. Impossible physical feats are achieved. The dead speak. But Brown delights in telling us that it is all trickery – a combination of sleight of hand, distraction, illusion, showmanship, fakery and audience manipulation. Like a number of other skilled illusionists, Brown achieves the apparently paranormal through simply being very, very clever.

But out there are a number of other very clever people who do not proclaim their illusionist skills as openly as Derren Brown. The history of psi and spiritual investigation is littered with a rogues' gallery of charlatans, confidence tricksters, fake psychics and dubious healers, all trading on gullibility and desperation. In the early days of psychic research, some con artists even fooled the scientific investigators of the Society for Psychical Research (it took stage illusionists to point out how easily the intellectuals had been duped).

These days, the murkier corners of the internet, the Z-grade satellite TV channels, the premium-rate telephone numbers, the back columns of tabloid newspapers, and pubs and clubs up and down the land are all happy hunting grounds for these predators. All kinds of tricks are employed, from obtaining information in advance on specific audience members and having 'plants' in the audience, to offering open-ended questions from the so-called spirit world ('Is there a John here? I have a message for John. Or Jack … ? Or Jim? Someone with a name beginning with J?').

A favourite trick is 'cold reading', where the 'psychic' makes instant guesses based on the clues we all give out – our age, social culture, accent, vocabulary, body language, hairstyle, mode of dress, even the perfume or aftershave we wear. For example, a woman twisting her wedding ring may be having marital problems; in an army town many people will be mourning loved ones killed overseas; and almost everyone of a certain age and class in a specific area will have a shared past, whether that is being affected by the Liverpool/Sheffield Hillsborough Football Disaster, or working in a local industry. People want to believe in the psychic world so much, they fill in the gaps, making it easy for the charlatans. As a general rule, the more money changes hands, the more suspicious you should be.

Chapter 3

THE SPIRIT WORLD

What happens to our souls when we die? Do we even have souls? Is there an afterlife? Do we remain as independent spirits or are we absorbed into some kind of collective consciousness? Will we meet up with our loved ones who have 'passed over' before us? Do any of the numerous and contradictory religions offer us the truth about life after death?

People have been asking these questions since the dawn of history. And despite spectacular advances in science, and the rise of several formal and informal belief systems centred on the notion that the dead are still with us and/or we can communicate with them, these questions still remain unanswered.

SPIRITUALISM: COMMUNING WITH THE DEAD

Spiritualism is the art of communing with the dead and while there are those who dismiss it as a Victorian parlour game with special effects, there are others who sincerely believe in it and who cleave to it as a comforting proof of the eternal life of the spirit. To those with faith, spiritualism is much more than a spooky pastime; in fact, it is a religion and is recognised as such by the British government. For those more sceptically minded, it can be seen as 'psychic Christianity'.

The Seven Principles of Spiritualism, as revealed to

Emma Hardinge Britten, a spiritualist pioneer, do not contradict a belief in a single, all-seeing God, nor the idea of a human soul being brought to account in the hereafter for conduct during earthly life.

The Seven Principles can be summarised as follows:

(1) God is the father of mankind.

(2) Humanity is one family; we are all each other's sisters and brothers.

(3) Communion with the spirit world is possible and desirable as spirits can offer us guidance and wisdom from 'the other side'.

(4) The human soul lives on after physical death.

(5) We each must take personal responsibility for ourselves and our actions.

(6) For our deeds on Earth, whether good or evil, we will receive compensation or retribution in the afterlife.

(7) Even after death, the possibility of redemption and spiritual progress is available to every soul.

Spiritualists believe that we are surrounded by spirits, though not everyone has awareness, not even every spiritualist. Only 'sensitive' psychic people can access this parallel universe and, even then, only through honing and developing their skills. These sensitives, who have become known as mediums because they serve as a channel of communication, usually discover their gift in early life, often during adolescence. They may encounter someone who has recently died, or a beloved relative, and have what appears to be a perfectly normal conversation with them.

Mediumship is an expression of the medium's personality and skills, and so not all spiritualist mediums work in the same way.

Mediums
Physical mediums

Physical mediums not only communicate with the dead, but also make their spirits visibly manifest. Helen Duncan, the famous wartime medium and the last woman ever to be tried under the 1735 Witchcraft Act, was a classic physical medium (see page 114).

Clairaudients

Other mediums operate on a less spectacular level, and often through choice. Albert Best for example (see page 98), was a *clairaudient*. That is, he transmitted the messages he received from the spirit world, often not understanding the implications or content of these messages but simply passing them on to their intended recipients.

Clairvoyants

Clairvoyants literally 'see' the spirits with whom they are in touch and are thus able to describe the appearance of the sender of the message. Some clients find it enormously comforting to be told that a loved one who died, for example, after being badly wounded in a war or as a result of a disfiguring illness is, in death, restored to their former selves.

Clairsentients

Clairsentient mediums can feel the emotional and sometimes the physical pain of those from the spirit world. For example by touching/feeling an object linked to a departed soul they can actually experience the pain and hurt that spirit experienced during their lifetime. Horribly, they may even experience how they met their physical end.

Clairomas

Clairoma mediums experience smell as part of their communication with spirits. This may be someone's pipe tobacco, or a special perfume.

Mediums who communicate through automatic writing

Some mediums use automatic writing as a form of psychic communication. In this case, the medium holds a pen and paper at the ready in order to allow the communicating spirit to convey its message through the medium's hand. The medium, driven by the spirit, scribbles fast and furious messages, which, like the spoken ones, are generally only explicable to the intended recipient.

Trance mediums

Finally, there are trance mediums, who appear to be taken over by the voices of spirits which speak through them. This form of mediumship, where odd, sometimes very strange, voices emanate from an apparently sleeping person, has led some to believe that spiritualism is, in fact, a form of demonic possession.

Sceptics

Most mediums are happy to deal with sceptics and agree that, after all, why should you believe something that you have never personally witnessed? They urge people to attend spiritualist meetings with an open mind. However, there are a number of questions that surface again and again with regards to spiritualism. One that is often asked is how can a medium be sure that the spirit with whom they are communicating is not malevolent and bent on imparting destructive messages? One answer is that not every spirit is a good one. Mediums do warn amateurs to beware of evil spirits, who can be called up easily enough (through séances and Ouija board sessions) but can prove much harder to get rid of. Most mediums have one or more spirit guides, who are there to ensure that 'lower' or malevolent spirits do not escape through the portal from the other side, i.e. the 'window' created temporarily by the medium during a sitting or trance.

Another question – or rather accusation – that is raised by sceptics is that mediums make statements that are so general they are bound to apply to someone in a large audience. Couple this with the fact that many mediums cannot always offer a name for a spirit, and it is easy to see the comparison with daily newspaper horoscopes, in which readers are given such nebulous information that practically any outcome would fit. An exception to the rule was Albert Best, a former postman, who was able to deliver personal details, including not only precise names but also addresses.

A further charge is that mediums seed their audiences with 'plants' so that even if the real messages prove vague and unconvincing, the psychic can fall back on a couple of sure things. This, the reasoning goes, ensures that audience members go away with the impression that the medium made meaningful contact with the other side, even if this time they were not lucky enough to be recipients. There is also the claim that mediums respond to verbal and nonverbal clues unwittingly given by audience members. For example, a young woman twisting a wedding ring could be a new bride experiencing marital problems. Or the medium could say he has a 'Dave' and an eager audience member will supply the full name, and even betray details of the relationship with him or her.

Studies of mediums have been conducted by, amongst others, the Society for Psychical Research, which was established in 1882 by a group of Cambridge scholars, with the express purpose of investigating paranormal activities in a rigorously scientific manner. Past presidents, including former British Prime Minister, A. J. Balfour, eminent physician, Sir William Crookes, and physiologist and Nobel Laureate, Charles Richet, testify to the high status of its membership. One such investigation, published in the *Journal* of the Society in January 2001 and conducted by Gary E. Schwartz, Linda G. S. Russick, Lonnie A. Nelson and Christopher Barentsen, considered the very issues just outlined. They hoped to ascertain whether a skilled medium really could obtain accurate and replicable information from the spirit world, or whether, indeed, they relied on the information they could glean from their sitters.

Five individual mediums took part in the investigation, along with one subject, who was unknown to them all. The subject, a woman from Arizona, had experienced six significant losses within the previous decade, and prior to the sittings, completed a comprehensive questionnaire detailing the circumstances and nature of her losses. Needless to say, the mediums were barred from conferring with each other. To eliminate the possibility of visual clues, the woman sat behind a screen during each sitting. And to eliminate the possibility of verbal clues, she was allowed to give only 'yes' and 'no' answers to any questions the mediums asked her.

Video cameras recorded each sitting and full, verbatim transcripts were made. The results were incredible. The study showed that the mediums achieved an average accuracy of 83%. The average accuracy for 68 control subjects, where chance was the only factor in play, was by contrast only 36%. In a further experiment conducted by the same team, accuracy levels were recorded at an average of 77%, leading the researchers to conclude that skilled mediums can indeed obtain accurate and replicable information from the spirit world.

Not everyone is convinced, some maintaining that other, as yet unknown, factors may be at work. And there are, unfortunately, enough fraudulent mediums at work to make anyone wary.

The Origins of Spiritualism

As far back as 540 BC, Pythagoras was interpreting messages from the dead, assisted by his student Philolaus. However, it took more than two millennia for communion with the dead to become a widely practised phenomenon. It is a curious paradox that, the more we progress in terms of technology, science and philosophy, the more we seem to be drawn to the inexplicable, to the realms of intuition, otherworldliness and spiritualism.

The Victorian era was one of unprecedented change, in which all the old certainties were being swept away by the impatient hand of modernity: traditional systems of labour were undermined and ultimately made obsolete by the new age of machinery; long-standing communities collapsed as people migrated to the now sprawling cities in search of work; religious tenets were contradicted by scientific breakthroughs; and the ancient and comforting idea of earthly life as a precursor to a heavenly afterlife went up in smoke. To those who recoiled from the new, seemingly soulless world, the strange tale of the Fox sisters must have been irresistible.

The Fox sisters

To explain the origins of spiritualism we must look at some events that took place in 19th-century New York State. Margaret and Kate Fox were two young, perfectly normal sisters, growing up in the small town of Hydesville, south of Buffalo, New York. The only extraordinary factor was that the house in which they lived was reputed to be haunted by the spirit of a travelling salesmen who had been murdered in their cellar many years before. This tale, however, was unknown to them initially, and the town records were a little sketchy.

The girls, then aged 9 and 11 years, were constantly troubled by knocking and banging sounds during the night. So much so that, on the night of 31 March 1848,

Kate attempted to communicate with the restless spirit. Urging 'Mr. Splitfoot', as she nicknamed the spirit, to do as she did, she clapped her hands twice. Mr. Splitfoot responded with two loud raps. Establishing a system of two raps for yes and one for no, the girls were able to conduct a coherent dialogue with their guest, who told them of his history and led them to a fragment of skull and hair interred in the cellar.

The girls' father called in the neighbours to testify to the veracity of these incredible events and word soon spread. Joined by their sister Leah, the Fox girls were soon embarking on spiritualist tours, where people gathered to witness their terrifying yet intriguing dialogues with the dead, who communicated through loud raps on the table top or by manipulating objects around the room. It began as a craze, an absolute must-see on a par with freak shows and circuses. But it grew to be much more than that. Naturally, it attracted the ire of the established churches. The Fox sisters, and those who followed in their footsteps, were subject to verbal and physical abuse and were denounced as ungodly and blasphemous. Yet, by the close of the century, spiritualism had elevated itself from the status of vaudeville to a serious religion with millions of followers.

Even more curiously, Margaret Fox, in later life, confessed that the events at Hydesville had all been a hoax. The knocking sounds – she now claimed – had been made by the girls themselves, who were adept at cracking their toes. The whole enterprise had started out as a prank to scare their mother and had simply got out of hand. Defenders of the spiritualist faith, however, point out that Margaret, by then a penniless widow and heavy drinker, was coaxed to confess by an enterprising news reporter offering a substantial fee. And in any case, in 1891, she retracted the confession. Furthermore, argued the faithful, how else could three unworldly young women have known about the murdered salesmen other than via a supernatural agency?

Spiritualism thrived in the teeth of its detractors and Margaret's confession, perhaps because it fulfilled a very human need – the need to communicate with the dead, and be comforted by the certain knowledge that everything did not end with the death of the body.

The Fox sisters inspired people across America. Their home town, which still has a plaque proudly commemorating the events as the 'first proof of the continuity of life, which was the beginning of modern spiritualism' is a hotbed of spiritualist activity and something of a pilgrimage destination for modern-day seekers of communion with their dead.

Emma Hardinge Britten and the spirit of Robert Owen

One of the many people inspired by the Foxes was the mother of the English-born Emma Hardinge Britten, then living in America. Thus, when the young Emma received an inexplicable message from she knew not where informing her that the ship she was awaiting – *The Pacific* – had gone down at sea, her mother seized on it as proof of a fledgling psychic sensibility. Emma, it seems, did not need too much coaxing and was soon sufficiently skilled in the art of mediumship to give readings to the public, including some in the company of Kate Fox.

Emma is perhaps most famous for being the recipient, in 1871, of the Seven Principles of Spiritualism (see page 95). These were received in a message from the spirit of Robert Owen (1771–1858), the great Welsh-born social reformer, best known for establishing the model village of New Lanark in Scotland. These Seven Principles became the foundation stone of the spiritualist religion and are still adhered to today.

Owen had converted to spiritualism late in life, following a sitting with an American medium called Mrs. Hayden, who travelled to Britain in the 1840s to become the first working spiritualist outside the United States. She was clearly a great hit. Indeed, she paved the way for spiritualism in Europe.

Meanwhile, poor Emma Hardinge Britten found she did not have the stomach for the vilification she received at the hands of America's religious communities and eventually she departed her adopted land for England, where the social atmosphere was already rather more tolerant. Her spiritualist career thrived and, as enthusiasm for this new phenomenon spread across the English-speaking world, she embarked on lengthy tours of both Australia and New Zealand. Her final claim to fame is that she founded the first weekly spiritualist magazine, *Two Worlds*, in 1887. The National Spiritualists' Federation, Britain's first official spiritualist organisation, was established shortly afterwards, in 1890.

The Victorian cult of death

Britain was perhaps more open to spiritualist ideas because of the Victorian cult of death. Queen Victoria, who reigned from 1837 till her death in 1901, was bereaved early in life and, many said at the time and still do so today, grieved excessively for her husband Prince Albert, who died in 1861. Retreating to her beloved Scottish home at Balmoral Castle, she wore full mourning for the remaining 40 years of her life and would have withdrawn from public life altogether if her Prime Minister had not warned her that such a move could imperil the standing of the monarchy in the eyes of the public. Was she the inspiration for her era's obsession with mortality? To an extent, certainly. This imposing figure – this sombre queen draped in widow's weeds – chimed with an age where, despite the dawn of major medical advances, infant mortality remained devastatingly high and life expectancy low. Death stalked everyone, even the very rich, even the Queen herself, and many attendant rituals were developed during her reign.

A widow was expected to mourn her spouse for a whole year, while a mother would mourn a lost baby for nine months, followed by three months of half mourning. The household clocks were stopped during the mourning period, and the mirrors draped in black crepe. Amongst the wealthier classes, tombstones and mausoleums became hugely important and many of the nation's most impressive cemeteries were constructed during the Victorian era. Death, far from being a taboo subject, became something that everybody lived with. The dear departed were remembered at every turn and from this sprang the age's fascination with post-mortem life.

Spiritualism did seem to offer something more concrete, in the form of direct communication with the dead. The traditional image of the Victorian parlour séance, with its wildly flickering candle flames, sinuous shadows and weird, disembodied voices, may set the hairs on the back of the neck on end, but their purpose was not to scare but to reassure and bring comfort. Spiritualism also had some social advantage over the established faiths. It was more inclusive, particularly of women, and less learned. Women, according to the beliefs of the time, were actually considered to be more conducive to the spirit world, and more likely to have psychic sensibilities. Unsurprisingly, spiritualism typically became known as the pastime of middle-class housewives, and the séance became a realm in which women, for once, were dominant.

Daniel Dunglas Home (1833–1886)

Of the early spiritualist pioneers, the name of Daniel Dunglas Home stands out. Born in 1833, this troubled young man grew up to become an internationally renowned physical medium whose demonstrations of levitation are the stuff of legend.

As an emigrant teenager in America, strange, poltergeist-like activity began to occur in the house he shared with his aunt. Furniture moved of its own accord, objects flew from one side of the room to the other, and odd, inexplicable noises were heard day and night. Poltergeist activity is often associated with unhappy youngsters and Home definitely fitted into that category, but this phenomenon had another cause, as his aunt was about to discover. She called in a priest, hoping he could exorcise the house of what she imagined to be some kind of demon. Instead he surprised her by deducing that the source of the problem was the boy's psychic abilities and that the solution was to control and develop his skills.

By the time he reached young adulthood, Home was an established medium on the spiritualist circuit. He travelled throughout the United States, holding séances at which tables would shake, vibrate and even lift off the floor and spirits would send long, complex messages through a code of sharp raps. Even more astounding were the hands that would miraculously materialise in mid-air and set about penning messages on the sheets of notepaper that were always available, and the musical instruments that would suddenly appear and play themselves. No wonder Home's appearances prompted eager queues round the block. And no wonder he aroused the suspicion of sceptics, eager to prove him a fraud. In 1855, Home returned to Britain, where he gave fantastic demonstrations of levitation and psychic communication at sittings in London, including some with the first of his calling, Kate Fox.

Home was a trance medium which meant that, upon commencing a sitting, he would fall into a somnambulistic state, from which he could only be roused very slowly. Whilst in one of these trances, on December 13, 1868, he performed his most famous demonstration of levitation. He was holding a sitting in London, in the top floor room of a patron's house. He entered his trance as usual and shortly afterwards, to the amazement of his onlookers, rose up bodily from his chair and sailed elegantly out of the open window. Outside, he hovered over the quiet, suburban street for some minutes before flying back through the window from whence he had come and returning to his seat. It need hardly be said that this event caused a sensation amongst the chattering classes of London and made the opponents of spiritualism even more determined to unmask him as the charlatan they believed he surely was. Step forward Sir William Crookes, an esteemed doctor and president of the aforementioned Society for Psychical Research. He approached his subject with the objectivity of the scientist and conducted a series of rigorous tests to ascertain, once and for all, the integrity of Daniel Dunglas Home. He found no evidence whatever of fakery or illusion and could only conclude that Home was either a man way ahead of his time in terms of trickery, or he was for real.

However, to this day there remain those who regard Home as a conman of the first order, pointing to his early retirement at the age of 40 as indicative of the fact that only a young man could pull of such convincing stunts. That said, even Harry Houdini, an arch-sceptic with, nevertheless, a long-standing fascination with spiritualism, could never replicate Home's incredible levitations and furniture movements.

Home died in 1886, of tuberculosis.

Arthur Conan Doyle (1859–1930)

Arthur Conan Doyle was born in Edinburgh in 1859 and is perhaps best known as the creator of the fictional detective Sherlock Holmes. But Sir Arthur, as he became after serving in the Boer War of 1899–1902, is also famous for being one of the great champions of spiritualism. Such was his faith in the endurance of the human spirit after death, and his enthusiasm for a religion that incorporated actual communication with these departed spirits, that he forfeited much of his credibility in the eyes of his peers and contemporaries.

Conan Doyle's early career as a doctor took place aboard various ships and in the towns of Plymouth and Portsmouth. However, he was also pursuing a parallel career as a writer and in 1887 and to enormous acclaim, published his first Sherlock Holmes story, *A Study In Scarlet*. In 1891, he was sufficiently successful to take the plunge into a full-time writing career and by the 1920s he was one of the most celebrated and highly paid novelists of his time.

In 1906, his first wife Louisa died. Then his son Kingsley, whose birth in 1892 he had described as 'the chief event' of his and Louisa's life, died of pneumonia during the First World War. Conan Doyle also lost his brother, two brothers-in-law and two nephews to this dreadful conflict. It was these terrible experiences that undoubtedly sowed the seeds of Conan Doyle's subsequent devotion to spiritualism.

The First World War

Interest in spiritualism had peaked in the mid-19th century, when it counted as many as 11 million devotees worldwide. But by the dawn of the 20th century, its popularity was already fading as the upper and middle classes found other amusements and the half-lit world of the séance began to seem hopelessly Victorian and old-fashioned. The fact that the spiritualist movement was disastrously disorganised and factionalised, and that the spiritualist circuit was awash with fraudsters charging extortionate fees and offering feats that would not have been out of place in a music-hall performance, further account for the movement's rapid decline. But the First World War changed all that, and prompted a huge revival of spiritualism, particularly amongst the working classes.

The 'War to End All Wars', as it was briefly known, broke out in 1914 and quickly became a world-scale conflict and arguably the most brutal war mankind had ever seen. Over 9 million were killed on the battlefield in the course of this four-year war, and as many again died as a result of genocide, starvation and bombing raids. As whole generations were wiped out at a stroke, hundreds upon thousands of women were left widowed with young children to raise alone. Small villages were left with no young men at all, farms struggled on without sons, industry without male apprentices. People lost count of the dead; it was slaughter on an unimaginable scale.

Thus it seems natural that these suddenly bereft, desperately grieving people would seek for a means of saying goodbye to the loved ones so rudely snatched away from them, and spiritualism offered them a route. The séance and sitting flourished during and after the War years, as mediumship again went into ascendancy. One of the primary attractions that spiritualism held for Conan Doyle was that, if it was true, then it meant his beloved son existed somewhere still.

From sceptic to believer
In 1894, having joined the esteemed Society for Psychical Research some years before, Conan Doyle, alongside Dr. Sydney Scott and Frank Podmore, took part in his first psychic investigation. A Colonel Elmore, living in Dorset, had reported a disturbing case to the Society. His wife and daughter, he said, had been hearing mysterious noises during the night,

including a rather chilling moaning call and the sound of chains being dragged along the floor by person or persons unknown. Not only that but the family dog now refused to enter certain rooms and most of the domestic staff had taken fright and left. Suitably intrigued, the three-man team spent a night attempting to record the 'fearsome noise' that ensued and to trace its source. It was certainly a hair-raising experience but their experiments were inconclusive. Conan Doyle, however, was convinced that something untoward and possibly supernatural had occurred. This gut feeling was compounded when, many years later, the long-deceased body of a ten year old was unearthed in the garden. The record does not show whether the Elmore hauntings ceased upon this discovery, but Conan Doyle was certain that it was the source of the disturbances.

Conan Doyle was also involved in further investigations, a series of which convinced him that telepathy existed between sympathetic souls. The death of his son accelerated his search and, a year later, he was rewarded when a Welsh medium brought forth a message from the young man. It was a profoundly moving and welcome experience and Conan Doyle believed firmly that it had been Kingsley 's voice he heard, speaking of 'concerns unknown to the medium'. Another time, he encountered his long lost mother Mary, and one of his nephews (who materialised before his eyes 'as plainly as I ever saw them in my life!'),thanks to the efforts of a physical medium. Sceptics, however, maintained that these were the distortions of a grief-stricken mind. In short, that Conan Doyle saw what he craved to see and nothing more.

In 1917, after much careful consideration, Conan Doyle went public about his belief in spiritualism. This public statement of belief was the scandal of its day, and caused many to think the poor man had gone mad. But even the most cynical concluded that, whatever the truth of the matter, Conan Doyle was sincere in his beliefs. Harry Price, one of the great investigators into psychic phenomena, who made it his business to unmask fakers and fraudsters – and a very profitable business it was too – said of Conan Doyle:

'His extreme credulity ... was the despair of his colleagues.'

Doyle and the Cottingley fairies

This queasiness in the face of Conan Doyle's convictions was exacerbated by the case of the Cottingley Fairies. In 1920, Conan Doyle was fascinated to hear of a series of photographic images taken by two young women, living in Cottingley, Yorkshire, apparently of fairies at the bottom of their garden. Elsie Wright, 16, and her cousin Frances Griffiths, 10, had taken a number of photographs of what appeared to be perfect little fairies, complete with diaphanous wings and tiny, doll-like features. Indeed, they so resembled the Victorian picture-book version of ladylike fairies, as opposed to the traditional Celtic image of rough, hairy folk with dark powers, that Conan Doyle should have known better.

Alas, he did not, and went so far as to publish an article in *The Strand* magazine describing the images as unquestionably authentic. Kodak film laboratories were not so sure. Though they confirmed that the images were neither double exposures nor had the negatives been tampered with, they were also able to confirm that the 'special effects' could be reproduced with ease. It seems that these two English girls had pulled a stunt that rapidly got out of hand. Sixty years later, they confessed, though their handiwork had long since been exposed as fakery – something of which most onlookers had not really needed convincing.

Houdini

That same year, Conan Doyle met the master illusionist Harry Houdini who had a huge (albeit at arm's length) interest in spiritualism. Following the death of his mother, Mme Weiss, to whom some say he was unnaturally close, Houdini was pitched into a welter of grief, from which he never truly recovered.

In the immediate wake of her passing, he sought out medium after medium, hoping to make contact with her. Instead he discovered, to his great horror, that most of the mediums he encountered were crude tricksters, more practised in the art of exploiting people's grief than communing with the dear departed. That set him off on another mission: to debunk spiritualism once and for all.

Surprisingly then, Houdini and Conan Doyle became great friends. Houdini was greatly appreciative of Doyle's open, honest and earnest personality, describing him as at least 'one intelligent person associated with this damnable art'. He asked Conan Doyle to prove that spiritualism was for real and the great writer naturally accepted the challenge.

Thus, in 1922, they met up in Atlantic City. Conan Doyle's second wife Jean was a psychic herself, transmitting messages from the other side through automatic or 'inspired' writing. She served as the medium at the ensuing séance, during which she contacted Houdini's mother, passing on her messages to her son in written English. Houdini was unimpressed. For a start, Mme Weiss, when alive, could not speak English, conversing in her native Hungarian right up until her dying day. Furthermore, she failed to mention to the medium that this particular day was her birthday; something that would never have slipped her mind during her lifetime!

Lady Jean attempted to dismiss these concerns, arguing that the messages of spirits are always transmitted in a language that the medium understands and that Mme Weiss would have little truck with birthdays now she was on the other side. This only incensed Houdini, who left the meeting deeply troubled.

The Conan Doyle–Houdini friendship was subsequently strained to breaking point when the former attacked the latter in the press, accusing him of actually being a medium himself, hence his zeal to debunk spiritualism. Doyle explained that Houdini did not perform amazing feats of human endeavour but simply achieved his escapes through 'dematerialising' in one place and 'rematerialising' in another.

Houdini responded angrily, saying Conan Doyle was 'senile' and continued in his crusade against what he considered to be dark arts, culminating in the publication, in 1924, of *A Magician Amongst the Spirits*, in which he exposed many of the prominent mediums of his day.

For his part, Conan Doyle was unshaken in his beliefs. He died in 1930 of heart disease, writing on the eve of his passing: 'The reader will judge that I have had many adventures. The greatest and most glorious of all awaits me now.'

Helen Duncan (1897–1956)

Born in the small, picturesque village of Callander, near Loch Lomond, in Scotland, Helen Duncan was to become one of the most famous physical mediums in history and was the last woman ever to be tried, and convicted, under the Witchcraft Act of 1735.

During her rather frugal childhood, she had a number of clairvoyant experiences, which her mother warned her not to speak about in public. An illegitimate pregnancy found her exiled to the jute mills of the industrial city of Dundee, where she met her future husband Henry, who had been invalided out of the army with rheumatic fever, an ailment that set the precedent for his future, chronic ill health. Like Helen, Henry was a 'sensitive' with a profound and intellectual interest in spiritualism. Because of his ill health, he was often unable to work. Instead, he devoted much of his time to reading spiritualist literature and using his accumulated knowledge to assist his wife in developing her skill. Times were very tough for this young couple. Helen endured no less than twelve pregnancies, from which only six children survived. She worked for a time in a local bleach factory, an awful, health-impairing way to make a living, while working as a medium in the evenings.

Like most of her clientele, Helen Duncan was a bitterly poor woman who struggled to survive. Dumpy, poorly dressed and matter-of-fact, she was like thousands of other working-class women, many of whom were left widowed by the First World War and thrown on their own resources at a time when women were paid substantially less than men for the same labour. Her mediumship offered solace in these bleak times, a glimpse not only of peace to come in the hereafter but a chance to speak to those who had passed over and to bask for a while in the past. Duncan was assisted in her work by her spirit guide, a rather snooty, elegant gentleman called Albert who nonetheless channelled a considerable array of otherworldly guests her way.

Can the camera lie?

Her mediumship was also, without doubt, a performance in itself. Once immersed in a trance state, ectoplasm would begin to emanate from her body, sometimes from her nostrils, sometimes her mouth. On one occasion, according to a witness, it actually seemed to 'spurt from the nipples of her breasts'. This alleged 'spirit stuff' would coagulate in mid-air, finally resolving into the figure of a spirit from the other side.

One photograph from a séance shows the spirit form of an elderly man, rendered visible by ectoplasm, which gives the appearance of his being draped in a thick white sheet. Though his body is pretty much entirely concealed, the details of his face are clearly rendered. This eerie figure seems to emanate from the side of the medium's head, to which it is connected by a kind of ectoplasmic umbilical cord. It has to be said that to modern eyes the ectoplasmic figures appear to be little more than crudely drawn faces attached to cheesecloth.

In demand

During the 1930s and 1940s, Helen Duncan began touring the country, hosting public meetings at spiritualist churches, village halls and private houses. As the Second World War began to ratchet up horrendous numbers of casualties, so the demand for a contact with the recently departed increased. At this time, estimates suggest there were upward of a million active spiritualists in Britain alone, over a thousand spiritualist churches and several thousand home circles, the latter being the smaller-scale, more domestic setting for a séance.

Wherever she went, Helen Duncan did not disappoint – the dead rose up before the living, imparting messages so detailed and accurate that onlookers could only gasp. How, they wondered, could this ordinary looking, middle-aged Scottish housewife be capable of such amazing feats? A widower called Vincent Woodcock attended one of Duncan's sittings, along with his sister-in-law, and was converted to spiritualism by what he witnessed. Helen Duncan did not merely pass on a message from Woodcock's dead wife, she caused the woman to materialise in their midst in a wave of ectoplasm. This phantom then took off her wedding ring and placed it on her sister's finger, saying: 'It is my wish that this takes place for the sake of my little girl.' All of which was music to the ears of Woodcock and his sister-in-law, who subsequently married, returning years later to another Helen Duncan séance. The dead wife obligingly reappeared, this time to bestow her blessings on the new union.

Major J. H. Webster MBE, in his book *Voices of the Past*, recounts two materialisations at the hands of Helen Duncan. In 1942, during the summer, the medium held a séance in Manchester at which a Mr. Ramsden, a Squadron Leader in the RAF, was in attendance. Though a keen student of spiritualism, he was yet to be fully persuaded as to its authenticity. The séance began as normal, with prayers and a hymn or two. The curtains were then drawn and Duncan descended into a trance. Within minutes, ectoplasm began to emerge from her body, forming an eerily opaque, moon-coloured cloud in mid-air. Gradually, the refined features of Albert, her spirit guide, began to distinguish themselves. He addressed himself, without ceremony or hesitation, to the startled Mr. Ramsden, who had booked himself in under a false name. Albert, it seems, was not fooled for a minute and announced that there was a woman waiting in the spiritual wings who was desperately impatient to meet with him again.

This woman transpired to be Mr. Ramsden's mother, who soon afterwards appeared, as if in the flesh. Rather tongue-tied at first, she confessed that, 'I have been waiting for this moment for years, and now I am here I feel too excited to know what to say.' Nevertheless, she did relate enough private family information to convince her son that what he was witnessing was more than a mere figment of his imagination.

Perhaps more startling still is the epilogue to this little story. In conversation with him afterwards, Helen Duncan revealed to Mr. Ramsden that she never saw the spirit forms herself, indeed had never seen a spirit form in her life. 'I am sure that if I did then I would die of fright,' she told him.

At a subsequent séance, in March 1943, Duncan accurately transmitted messages to what was a very international audience in a variety of languages of which she had no previous knowledge. Duncan had barely attended school, and gone to work very hard and very early; how could she therefore have a working knowledge, all of a sudden, of Afrikaans, a Bolivian Spanish dialect, Polish and Dutch?

At this same sitting, Duncan also brought forth the spirit form of a recently killed New Zealander pilot. His Wing Commander, a guest of Mr. Ramsden, could only gasp his astonishment.

Bill Watson, the deceased airman, went on to describe the nature of his death, pinpointing the cause to his inability to use his escape hatch. His Commander, suddenly regaining control of himself, demanded to know more and Watson was only too happy to oblige. His technical knowledge, the listeners insisted, far surpassed anything that Helen Duncan could have picked up. In fact, it is claimed that this Wing Commander later instigated a programme of modifications to the model of aircraft used by the tragic airman – along the lines suggested by Mr. Watson's ghostly debriefing.

A challenge

Mrs. Duncan took up the challenge laid down by Harry Price, the arch-sceptic, and former member of the Society for Psychical Research. He left this organisation to form his own, the National Laboratory of Psychical Research. Malcolm Gaskill, in his book, *Hellish Nell: Last of Britain's Witches*, describes the intrusive manner in which Price set about Helen Duncan.

First, two doctors were enlisted to conduct a physical examination, to determine whether she secreted objects or materials about her person. To all intents and purposes, it was as humiliating and invasive as the kind of strip-search conducted in prisons to ensure inmates are not carrying illegal drugs. Next, she was rudely awoken from a trance by someone shouting in her face. Meanwhile the ectoplasm that was beginning to emanate from her person was snatched for analysis. This analysis revealed Duncan's ectoplasm to be composed primarily of egg white and wood pulp while a series of X-rays revealed her incredible ability to swallow and regurgitate, at will, the materials required for her performances. Harry Price thus concluded that Duncan was 'one of the cleverest frauds in the history of spiritualism'. Duncan was deeply shaken both by Price's rough conduct and his damning conclusions. Yet the spiritualist movement was unshaken in its faith in her and the work continued.

Everything changes
But the event that was to turn Duncan's life upside down took place in Portsmouth, in 1941. The town was home to Britain's naval fleet and, as such, a target for the German Luftwaffe. Duncan called forth the spirit of a young sailor who explained to his attendant mother that he had been killed when his ship, HMS *Barham*, went down on November 25, 1941. Doubtless a strong dose of wartime hysteria infected proceedings because, in all likelihood, Duncan's mediumship was not half as accurate as people were later lead to believe. It is not beyond the realms of possibility that an anxious mother named the ship and that, when Duncan produced the son's name, they both put two and two together and made four. A warship sinking in wartime is hardly an

unwarranted guess. And almost certainly, the story grew arms and legs in the telling.

But the Admiralty had yet to release details of the sinking of the warship. Could Duncan, some wondered, be a spy? Suffice it to say that Duncan's activities were of enough concern to attract the attention of MI5, who were instrumental in building a case against her. So at a séance on the night of 19 January 1944, Helen Duncan was arrested and charged under the Vagrancy Act, later upgraded to one of being a false medium as per the 1735 Witchcraft Act, which expressly stated that witchcraft and communication with the dead *did not exist*. Under this ancient law, considered by most practising legal people to be all but obsolete, she was charged on the grounds that it was unlawful to 'exercise or use human conjuration that through the agency of Helen Duncan, spirits of deceased dead persons should appear to be present.' She was also accused of Larceny, 'by falsely pretending she was in a position to bring about the appearances of then spirits of deceased persons.' She was tried at the Old Bailey and, despite the attendance of numerous supporters as witnesses, was convicted and sent to jail.

Upon her release, and despite previously insisting that she would not, Duncan resumed her spiritualist career, though on a much smaller scale than before. The lurid publicity of the trial, coupled with the stain of incarceration, had tarnished her image in the eyes of the public. Not only that, but her psychic abilities appeared to be evaporating to the extent that the official spiritualist body, the National Union of Spiritualists, eventually revoked her license. Though she continued to scrape a halfway-decent living, Duncan was still subject to police raids, including one in Nottingham in 1956. Such was the shock she received on this occasion that she died five weeks later, aged only 59.

But the story does not end quite there.

Helen Duncan has allegedly made a number of notable appearances at modern séances, including one in which she apparently materialized before her daughter Gina, through the agency of the medium Rita Goold. She remains a revered figure within the spiritualist community, and is regarded by many as a martyr to the cause. On the other hand, it is clear from recent research that she often practised fakery at her séances, so she may have been both a charlatan *and* a genuine medium. Of such contradictions is a modern legend made.

Spiritualism Today

In the century and a half since spiritualism was established on any kind of organised basis, its public image has altered dramatically. The days of phantasmagoric materialisations, levitations through open windows and darkly clad dowagers holding hands in dimly lit drawing rooms are long gone, and the stormy dramatics that typically attended a Helen Duncan séance also seem to be things of the past. Sceptics may argue that the changes have come about because modern audiences are less likely to be convinced by crude theatrics such as ectoplasm and objects floating through darkened rooms. These days, a spiritualist gathering is a breezy, daytime affair with mediums who are matter-of-fact and often gifted with a sense of humour. The mysterious, amateur dramatics overtones may have gone, but it seems the popular fascination has not. The Spiritualist National Union now has in the region of 20,000 members in the UK, with three times that number estimated to be regularly attending Britain's 300-plus spiritualist churches.

EXORCISMS AND CLEARINGS

Many people have had recourse to exorcism or clearings to rid themselves of what they regard as a ghost or malevolent spirit. Exorcism, however, remains both confusing and controversial, and is not something to be taken on by well-meaning amateurs. For a start, there is often a problem with the very word. Most of what the press call 'exorcisms' are in fact much lower-order affairs, in which a Christian minister or priest will say prayers in the troubled home, or perform what is called a 'blessing', in which the official literally blesses the house in the name of Jesus. For those with religious faith, the use of holy words and formulae acts as a powerful force against the presumed malign spirit.

A real exorcism is a much more serious affair, in which the religious professional sets out to expel an evil spirit from a person – in other words, the troubled individual is regarded as being *possessed*. In Christianity and Islam, possession is typically believed to be caused by demons, while in Judaism and Hinduism the possessing spirit may be the ghost of someone who has died with business unfinished in this life, such as a murder victim. In practice demons and ghosts are just words that may be describing the same thing – for the exorcist, what is important is that the possessing spirit is unwanted, and must be persuaded to leave. The possession is usually characterised by extreme behaviour, such as violence against others, self-harm, fits and shakings, coarse language, invocation of demonic names, inappropriate sexual activity, vomiting, and speaking in unusual tones of voice.

The core problem for nonbelievers, of course, is that one person's demonic possession is another person's severe mental illness, and psychiatrists and therapists are usually aghast at the idea of invoking the supernatural in cases where patients are suffering from what they see as distressing but explicable illnesses. It should be remembered that, following the release of the film, *The Exorcist*, in 1973, there was a wave of exorcisms and illicit rites, some conducted by ordained ministers but others performed by occultists, fraudsters, and the simply inexperienced.

In the UK in 1974, two Charismatic Methodist ministers were involved in a horrendous case that quite rightly made most church people want to steer clear of this kind of activity forever. The pair had performed an extended, rather harrowing exorcism ritual within the church walls, on a man convinced he was demonically possessed. They then left him alone, thinking he was in an exhausted sleep. He woke, went home and, convinced his wife was the devil, bit off her tongue, causing her to bleed to death. In 1976 a German student, Annelise Michel, died in an exorcism, and in the 1980s the Islamic exorcism of a troubled Muslim teenager in the north of England led to another death.

For some Christians, exorcism is an acceptable practice because in the Bible Christ himself cast out demons. It remains an available option within the Roman Catholic Church, the Eastern Orthodox

Church, and a minority of Protestant traditions (very few in the UK, rather more in the USA). The Catholic rite of exorcism is a highly structured affair, and can only be conducted by an ordained priest with the express permission of his bishop, and only when mental illness has been fully ruled out. Very few actual exorcisms take place in the UK these days, although blessings are still common. 'Clearings' are sometimes carried out by some spiritualists, while those of a pagan persuasion may call in a Wiccan, Druid, white witch or other practitioner of benevolent magic. Some psychics regard troublesome spirits as entities that have become temporarily trapped between this life and the next; in this case the psychic may attempt to persuade the spirit to 'walk into the light', thus finding peace for themselves (and also giving peace to the living whose lives have been disrupted). The solution chosen very much depends on the belief system of the people involved.

In every case, it should be born in mind that there are a small number of unscrupulous individuals who are more than willing to exploit the distress of others: anyone considering asking for an unwanted spirit to be removed should be very cautious about whom they ask to assist.

NEAR-DEATH AND OUT-OF-BODY EXPERIENCES

In 2001 the medical journal *The Lancet* published a study from the Netherlands in which 334 patients who had been resuscitated after a heart attack were asked a series of questions about their experiences – 60 of them, or 18%, described what is now commonly termed a Near-Death Experience, or NDE for short.

Although the fine details varied, most of the descriptions bore a remarkable similarity, with the NDE following a standard pattern:

- A sensation of leaving the body, sometimes accompanied by the sound of something buzzing or ringing.
- Floating above the body and looking down on it (this part is often termed an 'Out-of-Body Experience' or OOBE).
- Moving through a tunnel or passage towards a distant light source, out of which emerge the spirits of deceased loved ones and/or religious entities such as saints or angels.
- A 'life review', in which the individual's good and bad actions are scrutinised as if they were watching them on a screen or tape.
- A sense of being 'pulled back' to the body, often accompanied by a message that 'it is not yet their time'.

Many of the patients said that the place they were in was so filled with a sense of love and peace that they were deeply disappointed to wake up again in a hospital bed. For most respondents the experience was positive, even profoundly spiritual, and some gained a new purpose in life, or renewed their religious faith. For a minority, however, the NDE was deeply awful, seeming to project them into a 'hell' rather than a 'heaven'.

Some spiritualists and members of other religious

groups have seized on this and other medical studies of NDEs as proof positive that the afterlife exists. Well, we know that NDEs can and do occur, but does this really imply survival after death? It is worth asking, for example, why 82% of the contributors to the Dutch study did *not* have an NDE.

Recent research means that we are beginning to understand the incredibly complex neurochemistry of what Fortean researcher Lionel Fanthorpe has dubbed 'the most mysterious object in the Universe – the human brain.' NDEs, it appears, may be brain chemistry in action, flooding the patient's crisis-ridden system with endorphin-like chemicals to dampen down pain and cope with the massive cellular damage of heart failure. The brain's visual cortex then seeks out images and emotions from the individual's 'data bank' of memories, and creates a hallucination-like internal experience partly based on the person's religious beliefs and upbringing. Support for this view comes from the attested situation that some psychotropic drugs can produce interior experiences very similar to NDEs, including the 'floating above the body' theme of the classic OOBE. In addition, OOBEs have been reported by people who are not in near-fatal conditions, such as in comas or under anaesthetic, and some meditation techniques are said to induce OOBEs and place them under conscious control, a process often called 'astral travel'. Shamans, sorcerers and mystics have often claimed they can send their spirit on long journeys out of the body. The present writer even once had an accidental semi-OOBE when he was sitting half asleep at his desk in warm sunshine.

So it may be that when the brain's chemistry is

stimulated in a certain way – either by trauma, or relaxation techniques, or by drugs – then an NDE-like experience can be created. Of course, it is notable that neither the majority of drug trips nor the majority of near-fatal heart attacks result in these kinds of experiences. So it may only happen under certain specific conditions that we do not as yet understand. It is also the case that, despite recent advances in understanding brain chemistry and the physiology of the dying process, no scientific researcher can tell us what will happen when we die. For the moment, the areas of conscious survival after death and the afterlife remain conclusively in the realms of religion and belief.

Chapter 4

EARTH MYSTERIES

The term 'earth mysteries' covers an eclectic mix of places and phenomena, with the core focus being on strange and curious things found on our planet, and especially physical monuments from the distant past. This typically involves ancient monuments, such as stone circles, but also includes ideas on how our ancestors thought about the landscape and interacted with it using religion, ritual and magic. 'Earth mysteries' as a field can embrace everything from serious archaeology and the folklore of sites to links with UFOs and psychic phenomena. In terms of earth mysteries, Britain is fortunate in not only having more stone circles than anywhere else, but also a concentration of the most unusual and enigmatic monuments anywhere in the world.

STONEHENGE AND OTHER STONE CIRCLES

There are more than 900 stone circles in the British Isles. Others are found elsewhere in Europe, and as far afield as Africa and the Pacific. They are often called 'megalithic' monuments, 'megalith' meaning 'large stone'. The most famous circle is Stonehenge, and it is the only circle with the famous Π-shaped arrangements, but many other circles are far larger, including the Avebury Ring at Avebury (Wiltshire), stone circles at Stanton Drew (Somerset), Long Meg and her Daughters at Little Salkeld (Cumbria) and the Ring of Brodgar at Stenness (Mainland Island, Orkney). The circles are wonderful, strange, enigmatic and compelling monuments. Not surprisingly, they have attracted speculation and odd ideas since the earliest times.

Over the centuries, the stone circles were supposed to have been built by ancient peoples such as the Egyptians, the Greeks, the Romans, the Phoenicians, the Trojans, the Danes, the Saxons and the Venetians. When ritual circles of timber posts were found in Plains Indian villages it was concluded that early Native Americans had constructed the British circles. In 1138, Geoffrey of Monmouth's pseudo-history *The History of the Kings of Britain* described how a race of giants originally built Stonehenge in Ireland, only for the monument to be magically transported across the sea by Merlin the Magician to suit the purposes of the mythical King Arthur. Geoffrey of Monmouth also tells us that Arthur's father, Uther Pendragon, was buried at Stonehenge, along with Arthur's cousin, Constantine, and his uncle, King Aurelius Ambrosius.

In more recent years, the idea has been advanced that the megalithic builders came from Atlantis. Atlantis was supposedly a highly technological ancient civilisation, destroyed in a great cataclysm on 12 August 3114 BC. According to this notion, the entirely mythical surviving Atlanteans arrived in Britain, where they used their mind powers and/or their advanced technology to erect the circles. Another idea popular since the late 20th century is that the circles, especially Stonehenge, are so complex and mysterious that the only people who could possibly have built them are our old friends, the extraterrestrials.

In contrast, and much perhaps to the disappointment of some people, we do know a fair amount about the culture that built the circles. They lived in Britain during the Neolithic and Bronze Ages, and started building circles in stone around 3300 BC. The first stage of Stonehenge was commenced about 3100 BC, which is 500 years before the Great Pyramid of Egypt was constructed. Although the circle builders did not have the wheel or iron tools, they used known technologies to move and erect many vast megaliths, an achievement that suggests centralised authority, determination, organised labour – and considerable intellectual skills. After more than two millennia, circle building ceased about 1000 BC. The circle architects left no writing behind, and when the first literate invaders (the Romans) arrived a thousand years later, the stone circles were already mysterious ancient monuments, their builders long forgotten.

As to *why* the circles were built, this is still debated, but archaeological digs at some of the larger sites are suggesting a multi-function purpose. In other words, the bigger circles may have been the all-in-one prehistoric equivalent of a cathedral, town hall, arena, dance hall and funeral parlour. Religious rituals were almost certainly conducted there along with feasting, dancing, civic meetings, ceremonies to remember the dead, and many of the other rites and gatherings that mark our lives. Above all, stone circles were functional, designed not only to impress but also to act as spaces for both sacred and secular ceremonies.

Of course that is not the whole story, as you do not

need to move 40-ton rocks a considerable distance just to have a nice place for worship, weddings and parties. The stone circles clearly had a ritual purpose. Unfortunately we know almost next to nothing about the religious beliefs of the prehistoric circle-builders. Did they venerate their ancestors, or regard them as supernatural guardians? Did they have a small number of gods, or a wide pantheon of deities? Did they worship the sun, or the moon, or storms, or trees, or the earth? Did they, as some tribes do today, regard certain stars as distant ancestors, the 'Adam and Eve' of their people? We do not know. But there is a strong hint that at least one stone circle was used in a specific ritual way – for magic.

Stonehenge is made up of two kinds of stones. The iconic ∏-shaped trilithons, composed of a horizontal megalith suported by two vertical stones, are light-grey 'sarsen' stones, sourced locally in Wiltshire. The much smaller and less noticeable uprights, called 'bluestones' because of a slight colour cast, come from the Preseli Mountains in southwest Wales, over 100 miles away. Archaeologists have now shown that these bluestones were selected from very specific sites on the mountaintops, locations that themselves are associated with other shrine-like structures, as well as springs that may have been regarded as sacred. The Preselis, then, may have had the status of 'holy mountains' in prehistoric times (holy mountains were important in ancient Greece, and continue to be venerated in India, Nepal, Tibet and Japan). The bluestones, when installed at Stonehenge, were seen as pieces of the holy mountain. In contrast to the giant sarsens, which once erected remained largely untouched, the bluestones were frequently moved from place to place within Stonehenge and the people who did the moving also frequently chipped off pieces of stone. Archaeologists Timothy Darvill and Geoffrey Wainwright have convincingly suggested that these chips were treasured as magical amulets designed to ward off illness. The bluestones were pieces of the holy mountain, and so the pieces of the bluestones were themselves holy, imbued with the magical power to heal. Intriguingly, in the 12th century Geoffrey of Monmouth described how pilgrims hoped to be miraculously cured by taking baths in water that had been poured over the bluestones, and in the 1600s visitors were frequently told that chips from the stones expelled diseases. Was this folklore that had survived for 2,000 years? Should we add 'hospital' to the list of Stonehenge's functions?

Stone circles may not have been built by aliens or by the Atlanteans, but they still have many secrets to be revealed. Archaeology is now moving at such a fast pace that any book on the subject that is more than 15 years old is already well out of date; and we can hope that many more megalithic mysteries will be unravelled in the near future.

THE DRUIDS

Every Summer Solstice groups of white-robed Druids turn up at Stonehenge. They conduct ceremonies, sport impressive beards, and get photographed a lot. Anyone watching their activities could be forgiven for assuming that this ritual had been in place since time immemorial, and that they were watching an authentic pagan rite from the distant past.

But it is not so. Modern Druids cannot trace their ancestry back beyond the year AD 1717, when the 'Ancient Druid Order' was invented by an 18th-century gentleman named John Toland; and 'ancient Druidry' was helped along by another colourful antiquarian called William Stukeley. Between the make-believe Druids of Stukeley and Toland, and the genuine Druids of ancient times, there passed at least a thousand years without anyone on the planet being called a Druid.

The Druids were the intellectual and priestly caste of the pagan Celts of Western Europe. They were described by Julius Caesar, who encountered them in Gaul (France), and brief mentions appear in the works of other Classical writers such as Herodotus and Pliny. When the Roman legions overran the Celtic tribes of Gaul and Britania, the Druids seemed to have become extinct. In Ireland, which was never invaded by Rome, Druids survived into the 6th century, where their pagan beliefs came into conflict with early Christian missionaries. From the few scraps of information that we have from antiquity and archaeology, it seems the Druids practised medicine, divination, and human sacrifice. Other than that, we know hardly anything about them.

Mixing together these pathetically few references with a powerful dose of wish-fulfilment and fantasy, the antiquarians of the 1700s invented a whole new Druidism, where the Druids were intellectuals, poets and artists – bearded and robed sages who advised kings and communicated with the gods. They were also, damn it all, *British*, without any of that Johnny Foreigner nonsense (the Druids of Gaul were conveniently forgotten!). Pretty soon toffs in London and elsewhere were dressing up in white robes and conducting 'Druidic' ceremonies, and the cult grew to the point that robes, a beard and a golden sickle (for cutting the sacred mistletoe) became the antiquarian equivalent of Masonic dress, to be worn during those 'special' ceremonies. Unlike the Masons, however, the Druids were more than happy to conduct their rituals under public gaze, and positive media reporting has been a consistent part of modern Druidry since the get-go. As an aside, several Welsh intellectuals also embraced Druidry, adapting it so that it was linked with the emergent Welsh nationalism, and Cornwall later borrowed and adapted the symbols of Welsh Druidry for its own brand of Celtic self-identity. These days Wales and Cornwall alike hold official celebrations in which all the honoured participants dress in Druidic robes.

In the 18th century, no-one had a clue who had built Stonehenge and the other stone circles. But with the 'ancient' modern Druids holding such a high profile, the link was there to be made. Soon it was accepted knowledge that the original Druids were the circle builders. Megaliths everywhere were renamed 'Druidic' stones, a term that still sticks in many locations. And the English Druids started to gather at Stonehenge during the Summer Solstice. The press started to take notice. By the time photography was invented, the white-robed Druids congregating beneath the great trilithons of Stonehenge were a photo opportunity just waiting to happen.

The only problem was, there is no actual link between the real Druids and the stone circles. The circles belong to the Neolithic and the Bronze Age, the Druids to the

Iron Age. By the standards of everything that is known today, the Druids are separated from the circle builders by at least several hundred years, if not longer.

Modern Druids are often active in the fields of ecology, environmental protest, conservation and the protection of ancient monuments. Their pagan beliefs underpin these important concerns, for they care about the past and about our fragile world. But any claims that they are founded on antiquity are bogus. Today's Druids are popular countercultural icons who provide a visual link to a past that remains important not just to aficionados of earth mysteries but to many who are interested in the wonderful history of our little planet. But as a belief system they are less than 300 years old, and their ancestors did *not* build Stonehenge.

LEY LINES

The popular idea of ley lines is that they are straight lines of unknown energy that link stone circles and other ancient sites. These invisible energy lines can be detected by dowsing, and their existence proves that ancient humans were in touch with cosmic or occult forces.

However, if ley lines truly exist, no-one has actually been able to demonstrate their reality. Like many areas of the paranormal, ley lines are a matter of *faith*, not of *fact*.

The idea originated in the 1920s with a Herefordshire photographer, Alfred Watkins, who noticed that ancient sites and historic churches often appeared to share the same straight line or alignment. Watkins suggested that these alignments were old travel routes, running straight from prominent site to prominent site for ease of navigation through the countryside. To describe these tracks he used the term 'ley', derived from an Anglo-Saxon term meaning 'open space', and went on to publish the classic work *The Old Straight Track*.

By the psychedelic 1960s, Watkins' straight leys, conceived of as physical routes used by traders and other travellers, had been transformed into something more esoteric – ley *lines*. Ley lines were invisible, magical, and mysterious: they were used by UFOs to navigate between stone circles; they were the nervous system of Mother Earth, and the standing stones were acupuncture needles inserted into the planet's skin in order to dissipate bad energies; they were an energy grid, connecting power nodes across the planet; they were grand patterns of cryptic sacred geometry, with straight lines stretching for many dozens if not hundreds of miles; they were other-dimensional connections that could only be sensed by those who had opened their third eye, or were vibrationally sensitive, or were psychic. They were marvels of space and time.

Or, possibly, they did not exist at all. Although these ideas are now part of popular thinking, and are endlessly recycled in journalism – especially in tourist brochures – the whole concept of ley lines is still stuck in the 1970s, and is well out of date. The chief problem is that ley lines cannot be objectively demonstrated: if you believe in them they are 'there', but if you do not, nothing exists to show you otherwise. They cannot be measured; they cannot be plotted on the ground; they cannot be seen, or touched, or revealed by instruments, optics or experimental procedures. At least Alfred

Watkins' leys were conceived of as physical routes, so we have something material to work with, something that can be shown to be 'real' or 'not real'. And although in most cases the long-distance tracks have proved to be illusory, a small number of short Watkinsinian leys do run as actual straight routes through the real world. In contrast, the esoteric ley lines only 'exist' if you believe in them.

Several of the leading adherents of ley lines from the 1970s, such as Paul Devereux and Danny Sullivan, both former editors of *The Ley Hunter* magazine, have recently pushed the field forward into new areas. Rejecting the airy-fairy notion of ley lines and the supposed linkage with stone circles, they have continued to investigate other straight-line mysteries. There appears to be a worldwide belief that spirits can only travel in straight lines, and research has identified a number of 'spirit lines' inscribed on the landscape in Scandinavia and North and South America (including the Nazca Lines – see page 142). These may be linked to ancient magical ritual practices such as shamanism. Also of interest are the medieval 'death roads' found in Europe and some 'church ways' in Britain, both of which were used for funeral processions and in some cases are dead straight. Sometimes the otherwise straight death road contains a deliberate kink – this is so the spirit of the deceased cannot return along the route and haunt the living.

Another area of cutting-edge research is what is known as 'cognitive archaeology'. Conventional archaeology has traditionally concentrated on *when* and *how* monuments were built. In cognitive archaeology, ancient monuments are studied not in isolation, but in relation to the landscape as a whole – the idea is to 'get inside the head' of prehistoric people and try to understand *why* they built a particular monument *where* they did. This approach has begun to reveal patterns that suggest ancient people conceived of some landscapes as sacred. A particular hill, for example, may have been the home of a particular god, or an ancestor spirit. Burial mounds may have been deliberately sited to show that the area was under the protection of the ancestors. Connections such as ceremonial routes were forged between the larger stone circles and nearby rivers and streams. Were these sacred waters? Caves, marshes and subterranean structures may have been conceived of as routes into the underworld.

Some stone circles were designed for ceremonies for the living but they may be surrounded by a complex pattern of burial places, thus creating a sacred landscape that was used for both religious ritual and veneration of the dead (an analogy may be a great cathedral that is primarily designed as a place of worship but also houses the tombs of the revered dead).

All this is now part of mainstream archaeological thinking, and so we have moved on from *imaginary* links between ancient monuments (ley lines) to *actual* links that are starting, however slowly, to reveal the thoughts and beliefs of the people who built the stone circles. Bear all this in mind next time you pick up a leaflet that excitedly talks about the 'magical ley lines' in the area you are visiting.

DOWSING

Some people claim to be able to detect ley lines through dowsing. Dowsers usually hold a pair of bent wires or hazel rods, one in each hand, and walk over a particular area. When the rods diverge or behave in unusual ways, this marks something unusual under the ground. Although critics say the movement is caused by micro-muscular contractions in the dowser's arms, many sceptical first-time dowsers find to their amazement that the rods do seem to move of their own accord.

On one level, dowsing really does work. We have ample evidence to show that some dowsers are able to identify underground water, metals and natural resources. Hard-headed German miners were using dowsing rods to locate minerals in the 1500s, and several modern companies employ dowsers to 'peer into the ground' in a search for obstacles such as service pipes.

But – and it is a big but – does 'energy dowsing' work? When we are dealing with tangible things, such as water, minerals or pipes, we can apply objective criteria: if the dowser says the water is at place X, and we dig and find the water there, then the dowser is vindicated, and if no water is forthcoming, the dowser's reputation takes a nose dive. But with 'energy dowsing' there are no objective criteria, because no-one can actually demonstrate the reality of ley lines or other alleged 'subtle energies'. Ley line dowsing is non-verifiable and so, once again, it comes down to a question of faith. If you believe in ley lines, you may be inclined to believe a dowser who claims to be able to trace one for many miles. But if you are disinclined to credit ley lines with much of an existence beyond the imagination, then don't invite an energy dowser to your next dinner party.

A little like telepathy and psychokinesis, dowsing

currently stands in a strange limbo scientifically speaking: we have evidence that it works, but we cannot identify *how* it works, what part of the human mind, body or perception is involved, or what mechanism is employed. And to make things more complicated, professional dowsers themselves cannot agree on what makes dowsing work, and the field is clouded by both New Age woolly thinking and outright charlatanism. Dowsing needs scientists brave enough to conduct a thorough research project, and dowsers willing to submit to full scrutiny. Perhaps only then will we understand more about this strange practice.

ASTRO-ARCHAEOLOGY

Also sometimes linked to ley lines is the field known as astro-archaeology (also called archaeoastronomy), in which some stone circles and other ancient monuments are said to be aligned on the setting or rising of the sun, moon or significant stars. The most famous astro-archaeological alignment is claimed for Stonehenge, and each Summer Solstice thousands of people turn up to see the sun rise. The only trouble is, this alignment does not actually exist, and the sun does *not* rise directly over the Heel Stone and into the main axis of the monument. Stonehenge is in fact astronomically aligned not on the midsummer sunrise but on the midwinter sunset (turn up on 21 December and if the weather is fine, you'll discover the truth of this).

Other ancient structures, from burial tombs in Ireland, Inverness-shire and Orkney to the major megalithic complexes at Callanish in the Outer Hebrides and Carnac in Brittany, are also demonstrably aligned on specific risings or settings of the sun or moon. It does seem, then, that the megalithic peoples were interested in the sky, and that possibly this was part of their religion. On the other hand, it has been seriously suggested by a variety of scholars that the circles were designed to study the sky in order to predict eclipses and recurring meteor showers, to determine the date to start planting crops, or to keep a count of the years and months. It is plausible that the circles were used both as calendars and for ritual/religious purposes.

But just to make this disputed area even more complicated, many stone circles demonstrate no astronomical alignments – in fact those that do have alignments appear to be in the minority. This is an area where cognitive archaeology may in the future provide more insights as we move from relating the location of monuments in the landscape to considering the entire three-dimensional space around the monuments, including the sky.

At present, however, astro-archaeology provides us with more questions than answers. Like so much in the realm of earth mysteries, the mysteries currently remain unsolved, although there is great potential for future work.

THE NAZCA LINES

Possibly the most mysterious and amazing lines on the planet can be found in the high and extremely arid desert of Nazca, in Peru. More than 300 shapes have been created on the desert plain. Most are criss-crossing straight lines, some of which stretch for miles, but others are astonishingly complex shapes representing monkeys, birds and spiders. The enormous figures can only be seen from the air, and were unknown to the West until flights began over the area in the 1920s.

The *how* of the Nazca lines is easily answered, as they were made by clearing the loose stone cover to expose the pale desert sand beneath. Although requiring enormous labour and elaborate planning, the process is not mysterious. The questions of *when* and *who* are also known quantities, as most of the lines date to the time of the Nazca culture (200 BC–AD 600). But the big mystery is *why*. Leaving aside Erich von Däniken's fanciful idea that the lines are UFO landing strips (see page 176), we are left with a mix of enquiry among the native population, anthropological comparisons with similar peoples, and educated guesswork – all of this pointing to the simple idea that we are dealing with religious beliefs.

The lines may have served two functions. The animal shapes may have been intended to be observed by the gods in the sky. Perhaps the shapes were symbolic offerings or sacrifices, or possibly they represented the gods themselves. The straight lines, meanwhile, seem to be connected to shamanic practices. Shamanism is an ancient religious practice found all over the world, and which continues to be practised in Amazonia, Australia, Siberia and parts of Africa. Shamans seek to alter their consciousness by engaging in rituals such as fasting, self-flagellation, chanting, repetitive dancing, and the consumption of hallucinogenic substances. In their 'altered state' the shamans allow their souls to fly to the 'otherworld' or the realm of gods and spirits. There they perform spiritual tasks, such as bargaining with a powerful spirit so that a member of the tribe will recover from a serious illness, or seeking out a tutor spirit to teach them further magical skills. The spirits the shamans consult often show themselves as animals or birds. When 'travelling' in spirit to their magical destinations shamans frequently speak of flying over the landscape in straight lines, and it is thought the Nazca Lines are 'spirit lines', designed to mark the mystical routes followed by the shamans' aerial spirits. Similar, although much smaller, straight lines have been found marked out on the landscape in other parts of the world, and the current consensus is that these too are spirit lines. It is easy to see a connection between shamanic 'astral travelling' and the out-of-body experiences described in the chapter on the Spirit World (see page 125).

It should be said that although the spiritual and shamanic explanations are plausible, nothing has been established for certain, and the Nazca Lines still remain one of the most mysterious sights on earth.

FAIRY PATHS

There are a number of places, especially in Ireland, where the human landscape has had to accommodate the acknowledged reality of the fairy world. Fairy paths are said to be used by the Good Folk when they travel from one base to another. As with the shamanic lines of South America, the fairy paths always run along straight lines. On at least one occasion a corner had to be shaved off a house because it infringed on a fairy path. In other areas doors had to be left open on either side of a barn because it too was on a fairy route.

These traditional beliefs have sometimes come

into conflict with the demands of a modernising Irish economy. In 2002, a single hawthorn tree at Latoon, County Clare, became the focus for a protest when plans were announced to build a road over it. The Latoon tree was widely regarded as a stopping point on a fairy path. Eventually the tree was saved, only to be vandalised by chainsaw-wielding idiots in 2003. Fortunately, new shoots have appeared, and the fairy tree should survive.

SILBURY HILL

It is 130 feet high and 550 feet in circumference. Something like 700 men labouring over 10 years shifted 240,000 cubic metres of chalk and soil to build it, using only tools of stone, wood and bone. It is a 9-sided truncated cone that some think bears a resemblance to a pyramid. It was constructed around 2600 BC and is one of the largest and most impressive prehistoric earthworks in Europe. 'It' is the majestic, mysterious and marvellous Silbury Hill, and we have no idea why it was built.

Silbury Hill is situated near the great megalithic complex of Avebury in Wiltshire, with its enormous stone circle and enigmatic stone avenues. Entirely man-made, the conical Silbury hill remains one of the most unexplained of all our prehistoric sites. The obvious function for such a labour-intensive monument would be a tomb for a king or someone of similar status. But several archaeological excavations have found nothing that even hints at a burial. There are no obvious religious features, such as shrines or patches of burning where feasts or sacrifices may have taken place. There are no artefacts. It took the best part of a generation to build, but we still do not know *why*.

But even in our general ignorance, new information comes to light. In 2010, archaeoastronomer George Currie, along with megalithic researchers Steve Marshall and Pete Glastonbury, discovered a phenomenon at Silbury called a 'sun roll'. (The angle of the rising or setting sun matches the slope of a hill, so the sun appears to slide or 'roll' up or down the side of the hill.) Over a period of some 30 minutes the sun rolls down the slope of Silbury Hill. The phenomenon only occurs twice a year, and is observable from two locations only, one of which is marked by a small prehistoric mound jokingly dubbed 'Silbaby'. The discovery was published in *Time and Mind: The Journal of Archaeology, Consciousness and Culture*, a publication at the forefront of the cognitive archaeology movement.

No-one is suggesting that ancient Britons built a massive nine-sided hill simply so they could have a nice view of the sun 'rolling' down its slopes a couple of times a year. What we do not know is whether the prehistoric builders noticed the phenomenon, and if so, whether it meant anything to them. Many of the larger stone circles are associated with the confluence of rivers, leading some researchers to suggest that water was sacred to the circle builders. The Silbury sun roll ends with the sun setting 'into' a natural spring. Did this accident of astronomy and geography give this spring a sacred quality? What mythology was constructed out of these events? Was it seen as a blessing of the gods? Or a descent of the sun god into a watery underworld? We will probably never be able to replicate the exact thinking and beliefs of our ancestors. But it is an odds-

on certainty that Silbury Hill has many other lessons
to teach us.

CHALK OR HILL FIGURES

The southern downlands of England are home to the
world's greatest concentration of giant figures, also
known as 'geoglyphs'. In most cases the topsoil has
been removed to reveal the white chalk underneath,
which allows the shapes to be seen over many miles –
indeed, so large are the figures that you need to be some
distance away to be able to appreciate the image. Most
of the figures were cut in the 18th or 19th centuries,
and the vast majority of them are white horses. During
the First World War various regiments also carved out
enormous representations of their cap badges. Some of
the figures, however, are much older – and much more
mysterious.

The oldest may be the Uffington White Horse,
in Oxfordshire. Unlike the stolid, solid horses of the
1700s, this is a beautiful, dynamic rendition of an
animal in movement, created in a stylised, almost
abstract manner. In fact, it may not even be a horse
– one intriguing suggestion is that it represents the
dragon killed by St George. On nearby Dragon Hill
lies a patch of ground where the dragon's blood was
supposedly spilled – and hence no grass will grow on
the spot. An earlier, now discredited, belief was that it
was created to mark the victory of Alfred the Great over
a Danish army in AD 878. The current theory, based on
archaeological dating, is that the horse was cut as long
ago as the Bronze Age (between 2000 and 800 BC),
and is a representation of either a horse goddess or the

local tribe's magical animal totem. The 'deity' idea gains credence from the fact that the 350-foot-long figure can only been seen from far across the vale or from the air – and the sky is the abode of the gods.

The extraordinary Cerne Abbas Giant in Dorset is portrayed with eyes, eyebrows, mouth, ribs, nipples and genitals, and is also carrying a huge club two thirds its own height. Expressive and powerful, the great figure is currently undateable, although popular belief, even among archaeologists, is that it represents the semi-divine mythological hero Hercules, whose great strength (and his tendency to use a tree trunk for a club) made him popular with the Roman army. Perhaps a local Celtic tribe mixed their own war-god with Hercules and created the carving. Because of the figure's obvious virility, there is a longstanding folklore tradition that spending the night on the hillside promotes fertility. The Giant is an astonishing 180 feet tall. But even taller, with a toe-to-tip height of 229 feet, is the Long Man of Wilmington, in East Sussex.

This featureless outline figure holds two upright 'poles' in its outstretched hands. The Long Man is the most enigmatic of all British hill figures, because it has changed so much over the centuries. It is now outlined in brick, rather than chalk and some distinguishing features have been lost. Were the 'poles' once spears, scythes, symbols of office, or even doors? What did the now-gone helmet and face look like? All attempts to date the monument have been equally frustrating, with speculation from the Neolithic (before 2000 BC) to the Celts, Romans, Saxons, early Christians and others – all finding no supporting evidence. At present the best guess is that it might be only 400 years old, but even that is disputed. As to what the figure represents, once again we are in the dark. Viewed from anywhere on the ground it is foreshortened and distorted, and the best place to see it is from the sky, so perhaps it depicts a god.

The figures at Wilmington and Cerne Abbas are today Britain's only giants, but once upon a time several more chalk-cut behemoths strode across the English countryside. The giant at Plymouth, called Gogmagog (or possibly two giants called Gog and Magog) and also carrying a club, lasted until 1666. There was another Gogmagog near Cambridge, and the Shotover Giant in Oxfordshire. All may have dated, like the Dorset figure, from the Celtic Iron Age. Sadly all these giants, including their exact locations, have long vanished. Elsewhere in the world, a giant hammer can be found carved near to Tours in France, with an eagle in Hungary, a white horse in North Africa, and other figures in the Rocky Mountains and in Chile's Atacama Desert. And closer to home, there is an 18th-century horse and stag on Mormond Hill in Aberdeenshire.

CUP AND RING MARKS

Ancient bowl-shaped depressions called 'cup-marks' and 'rings' of concentric circles, spirals and grooves can be found on natural boulders and rocks as well as on the stone megalithic monuments of Britain, Ireland and Europe. This beautiful and abstract prehistoric rock carving was created during the Neolithic and Bronze Ages (3300–800 BC) by people who had no writing to tell us what the enigmatic shapes mean. The rock carvings took immense labour to create and so were clearly very important to those who made them; but despite centuries of learned speculation we have no real idea what the symbols mean.

Many archaeologists have proposed an entirely practical purpose for the carvings, from tallies of livestock animals and directional signposts to markers claiming tribal territory ('Keep Out! We Live Here!').

Other suggestions are more esoteric, including star maps of the night sky, 'family trees' of nobles or chiefs, indicators of where to find good water, and two-dimensional sketch maps of the surrounding terrain or tribal boundaries. Another possibility is one popularised by writer Graham Hancock in his book *Supernatural – Meetings with the Ancient Teachers of Mankind.* Drawing on the work of anthropologists who have studied ancient cave and rock art in southern Africa, South America and Mediterranean Europe, Hancock speculates that the 'dots' and 'rings' are representations of shapes that appear before the eyes during hallucinogenic experiences (such as those associated with shamanism). Drawing on many other examples, Hancock suggests that the purpose of much ancient art carved on rocks and monuments is to represent the visionary experiences of shamans under the influence of psychoactive substances. He goes even further when he wonders if ancient shamans generated 'altered states' so they could communicate with paranormal intelligences from other dimensions or levels of consciousness.

Few archaeologists will follow Hancock that far. And the rock carvings on British stone circles and boulders may have nothing in common with the more elaborate carvings found elsewhere. But prehistoric rock art remains one of the great puzzles of our ancient landscapes, and the enigmatic carvings continue to fascinate and bamboozle professional archaeologists and amateur 'earth mysterions' alike.

SEAHENGE

One of the most remarkable and mysterious recent finds from the ancient world came in 1998, when low tides on the Norfolk coast exposed a circle of more than 50 upturned oak trunks surrounding a central object – an entire upside-down oak tree. Dubbed 'Seahenge' because of its location, the tree circle had not originally been erected anywhere near the sea, but over the millennia the low-lying coast has been eroded. The site is utterly unique in British archaeology because organic materials, such as wood, do not usually survive for thousands of years. Because of the vulnerable location all the timbers were removed for preservation and the circle has now been re-erected in the Lynn Museum in Kings Lynn. The circle has been dated to the Bronze Age, at around 2000 BC.

There were no clues to show why the tree circle had been erected, but archaeological sites elsewhere and anthropological studies of religious practices among non-industrial peoples today, may give us hints. The first suggestion is that this was a burial site, with the body of a prominent person deposited in the central oak tree. Over time the corpse would decompose and the site would remain dedicated to the individual's memory – a practice still found today in some tribal societies. The other possibility is that it was a shrine to a god, or a deity associated with trees. It equally could have been both sepulchre and shrine or neither, for the religious beliefs of the people who lived 4,000 years ago in Britain are unknown to us. We also do not know why all the trees were upside down – was this simply because it was more practical to work like this, or was there a ritualistic reason? As with so much of our ancient past, the archaeologists can tell us only so much, but the complex motives and beliefs of our ancestors remain elusive and mysterious.

Chapter 5

EXTRATERRESTRIALS

THE COMING OF THE SAUCERS

The modern UFO age began on what was an otherwise unexceptional day on 24 June 1947 when fire equipment supplier and private pilot, Kenneth Arnold, made a business flight past Mount Rainier in Washington State, on America's northwest coast. At a height of 9,200 feet he spotted a formation of nine crescent-shaped objects that were reflecting the bright sun. An experienced pilot, he had never seen their like before, and reported the sighting when he reached ground. In an interview with a local pressman he described the craft as moving 'like a saucer would if you skipped it across water'. In using these words Arnold was attempting to describe how the craft *moved*, but the report was mangled and soon headlines were mistakenly describing the *shape* of the objects as 'saucers'. The misquoted phrase 'flying saucers' was born in a blaze of publicity, and the world was never the same again.

Within weeks flying saucers were part of everyday culture in the USA, from workplace gossip to sensational newspaper stories, cash-in books, and, soon, an entire raft of B-movies. Within the wider world, both America and the Soviet Union were using rockets in an attempt to put a craft into space (the Russians succeeded in 1957 with the world's first satellite, Sputnik 1). As the

Cold War hotted up, America looked to the skies and saw a different kind of invader – flying saucers piloted by hostile aliens. Culturally, the saucers are still with us, as shown in everything from films, such as *Independence Day*, to the covers of science fiction books.

Kenneth Arnold often attempted to correct the original 'flying saucer' mistake, insisting that he had seen 'flying crescents', but the idea was too firmly rooted in popular consciousness to be shaken by mere facts. Arnold also realised his own previously unremarkable life had now been touched by the strange. He became, in effect, the first private UFO investigator, interviewing other Americans who claimed to have seen saucers and other 'alien craft'. He also coauthored a book on his experiences, entitled *The Coming of the Saucers*, and went on to claim around a dozen or so more sightings.

Arnold's original experience has been picked over by UFO historians. Although he originally estimated the nine craft were travelling at high speed more than 100 miles away, a US Air Force investigation concluded that the objects were in fact much nearer, and moving quite slowly. Given that Arnold had first been distracted by the sunlight reflecting off the objects, suggestions have been made that he had actually seen high-altitude snow, or a missile, or just reflections from the canopy of his single-engine plane. One very plausible notion is that the 'crescents' were in fact a flight of pelicans. We will probably never know the real truth.

The summer of 1947 saw a wave of reported saucer sightings, although in official documents they were described as 'flying discs'. By 1952 it was plain that most sightings were not actually of saucers, but of a wide variety of shapes and structures, and so the US Air Force investigation, Project Blue Book, substituted the neutral term Unidentified Flying Object or UFO. Strictly, this refers to anomalous objects in the sky that appear not to be natural weather phenomena or man-made craft; in practice, 'UFO' has become a synonym for 'alien spacecraft', although the acronym does not actually imply this. The implied link between something strange seen in the sky and alien visitors is the basis for what is known as the Extraterrestrial Hypothesis or ETH. Although other paranormal notions have been put forward for UFOs, from mental projections and ghosts to entities from alternative dimensions or visitors from the future, the ETH remains the dominant ideology.

THE ROSWELL 'UFO CRASH'

> 'The intelligence office of the 509th bombardment group at Roswell Army Air Field (RAAF) announced at noon today that the field has come into possession of a flying saucer.'

That was the story in the *Roswell Daily Record* on 8 July 1947. The accompanying headline in the small New Mexico paper read: 'RAAF captures flying saucer on ranch in Roswell region.' It was just a few days after Kenneth Arnold's experience had catapulted the phrase 'flying saucer' into the American consciousness. Here there was an official pronouncement from a military source that not only were saucers real but one was in American hands. Within hours Roswell was a media sensation. The Pentagon clamped down, swiftly issuing a press release that the 'saucer' was in fact the wreckage of a weather balloon. Most of the press accepted the cover story, and the Roswell 'saucer crash' faded away for thirty years, but these days Roswell is the most famous UFO case in the world.

Of all the toxic and bizarre ingredients in the UFO soufflé, none has a stronger taste than the mix of UFO lore and US military secrecy. Without the association with official bodies, the entire UFO experience could be dismissed as a mass of misidentifications garnished with a significant amount of looney wish fulfilment. But from the very start of the flying saucer era, the American military complex was deeply implicated in the expansion of what might be termed 'the aliens are coming to get us' culture. Of course, the Pentagon wasn't going round claiming little green men were abseiling into America – they were more concerned about keeping alleged Russian secret weapons under surveillance, while ensuring their own top secret projects went undetected (and unreported in the US media). But the Cold War made American hawks jittery, and so the whole 'flying saucer' episode had to be investigated just in case it turned out to have a Soviet element. But it is this involvement of the US military – with all the implications of status and power – that has enabled 'ufology' to endure for so long, and to capture the public imagination via the popular media. Roswell is the perfect combination of the military–UFO nexus, and since its 'rediscovery' in the 1970s it has spawned numerous books, several films, a mention in *Star Trek*, the core mythos of *The X-Files*, the teen TV series *Roswell High* and the alien conspiracy drama *Dark Skies* – among others. And it all happened by accident.

William 'Mac' Brazel, a foreman on a ranch 80 miles north of Roswell, had heard an explosion on the night of 2 July 1947. The next day he found scattered debris, which seemed to consist of flimsy pieces of wood, some silvery foil-type substance, and paper or parchment containing what might have been a form of writing. On 6 July Brazel took some of the pieces to the Roswell Army Air Field, and the remainder of the debris was picked up the following day. The base hosted not only conventional long-range bombers, but also a research project into rockets and nuclear weaponry. Despite this, no-one recognised the debris, and the genuinely puzzled RAAF team, no doubt influenced by the recent furore over flying saucers, issued the now notorious press release.

Over the ensuing decades an entire modern mythology has evolved around the incident. The core myth is: (1) an alien spaceship crashed at Roswell; (2) bodies were recovered from the crash; (3) the first press release was a genuine and honest description, which was later obscured by a series of cover-ups and conspiracies; (4) the alien corpses and the remains of the ship were shipped to Wright Field, Ohio (later called Area 51) which became the US centre for extraterrestrial research; (5) the US military has been reverse engineering the alien technology ever since, leading to weapons and propulsion systems so secret even the President is not told about them; and (6) the dead aliens were autopsied and the results filmed, the secret footage being leaked to an agog world in the 1990s. And, despite acres of newsprint, numerous Freedom of Information requests, conspiracy theories galore, and umpteen revelations from alleged 'men-in-the-know' coming forward to finally breathe the truth on television documentaries, no-one has ever demonstrated the reality of a single one of these extraordinary claims.

Roswell was the seed from which has sprung a tree with a thousand branches. The small desert town now attracts thousands of UFO enthusiasts every year, and the local road is known as the Extraterrestrial Highway. But what really happened in 1947? There has been so much subterfuge, hoaxing and confusion that it is tempting to suggest the real story will never be told. However, a US government investigation of 1995 might have uncovered the truth. The infamous debris found on 'Mac' Brazel's ranch was indeed from a balloon – but not an ordinary weather balloon. It was in fact an experimental set of instruments designed for high-altitude monitoring of nuclear explosions – specifically, of Soviet atomic weapons, which up to that date had not been tested. As such the entire project was top secret, and since the balloon had not originated from RAAF, none of the staff at Roswell recognised the wreckage.

Once the 'flying saucer' story hit the newswires, the Pentagon realised their covert toy was about to be made public, so they instituted a cover-up, even going so far as to publish photographs of faked debris from a real weather balloon. If the night of 2 July 1947 had not been a stormy one, had a weather-tossed secret device not plummeted to earth on a remote desert ranch, and had an impetuous military public relations officer not sent out a speculative press release, then no-one in the wider world would ever have heard of Roswell.

UFOS BEFORE THE SAUCERS – PHANTOM AIRSHIPS, FOO FIGHTERS AND GHOST ROCKETS

Strange sightings recorded as dragons, witches, demons and other supernatural entities have been seen in the sky since records began. It is only in the late 19th century, however, that we find the first mass reports of anomalous aerial phenomena – and they were not regarded as alien spacecraft, but as airships built by crazed inventors or malign foreign powers. Simple balloons had been known since the 1700s, but the first powered airship flight did not take place until 1852. This revolutionary new technology caught the public's imagination (not to mention the attention of early science fiction writers such as Jules Verne, who included futuristic airships in his influential novel *Robur the Conqueror*). Airship development, however, was painfully slow, and by the 1880s and 1890s the craft were still sluggish and unreliable machines capable of only short flights. Yet during those decades, hundreds of reports came in from the United States, not only of large, fast-moving mystery airships but also of their passengers – who were usually 'foreign' in some way, speaking or leaving documents in an unknown language. In some cases, airships hovered over specific locations while their aviators clambered down rope ladders to inspect the countryside and take notes.

A similar 'wave' of airship sightings came from as far afield as New Zealand, Argentina, South Africa and the remoter parts of Europe. In many cases, the reports were newspaper jokes or deliberate jokes, and in the new world of mass communications, stories could easily and quickly pass from one newspaper to another, to be 'adapted' with local details for local consumption. Others are less easy to explain, although the list of natural IFOs on page 166 may provide some candidates. But what is certain is that none of the reported airships ever existed.

The mystery airships were back in 1912, this time over the shores of Kent. The same year, Germany had successfully flown the first Zeppelin, and, with war looming, the British government were genuinely concerned that military airships carrying bombs could cross the Channel. In 1913, Zeppelins were spotted over Liverpool and Hull. And when the First World War broke out in August 1914, enemy airships were reported from every part of the country, including the far northwest of England and Scotland – many miles from Europe. Ufologists have dubbed these mystery aircraft 'scareships', because they seem to be mere phantoms of war fever. The Zeppelins did not have anything like the range to reach anywhere in Britain until 1915. Even later in the war, Liverpool, Carlisle and Barrow-in-Furness would all have been beyond their limit – yet all three strategic locations were consistently reporting sightings of enemy airships.

These false sightings must be put in the context of the times – not only was there widespread fear that an 'air war' would rain death and destruction down on Britain, but in 1914 everyone 'knew' that a major naval battle had been fought in the North Sea, and kept secret. Witnesses described hearing the blast of guns and seeing the distant explosions, while mariners reported the wrecks of damaged warships. Needless to say, the engagement had never taken place – like the scareships, it was just another myth of the war.

Another world war brought a different kind of proto-UFO. 'Foo fighters' were luminous balls of light seen on a regular basis by Allied aircrews from 1940 to 1945. The mysterious globes would appear close to the bombers or fighters but then move away, often performing manoeuvres impossible for any normal craft. The name came from a cartoon character whose catchphrase was 'Where there's foo there's fire.' The initial idea was that they were some kind of Nazi secret weapon, but the globes never touched or damaged the Allied aeroplanes, and they didn't behave like artillery flak. One of the truly strange things about foo fighters is that they were frequently reported during the Second World War, but not since – and then exclusively by Allied crews during the conflict.

Although they are probably some kind of electromagnetic phenomenon, at present foo fighters remain one of the unsolved mysteries of the Second World War. These days, the name is used by a popular heavy rock group.

The early days of the Cold War brought the final group of proto-UFOs to public attention. In the summer of 1946 almost 1,000 rockets or missiles were reported from the skies over Finland and Sweden. The reports caused a panic – it was feared that the Soviet Union was firing long-range V2 rockets captured from Nazi scientists, and that the launches were the harbingers of a new conflict. As an official investigation at the time found, however, it could not be proved that the 'ghost rockets' ever actually existed. Almost certainly, most of the sightings were misinterpretations, fuelled by war panic, of an exceptionally bright series of meteor showers.

UFO 'WAVES'

In 'ufological' terms, a 'wave' is a concentration of UFO reports, usually in a short space of time, and often limited to a geographical area. The scareship sightings mentioned above could be seen as the very first wave. The first 20th century wave took place in the weeks following the seminal events of 1947. The next one hit Washington DC in 1952, and was the event that turned US government interest in the UFO phenomenon from mere involvement to near obsession. The start of the wave was truly astonishing, with a strange fast-moving light buzzing a garden party in Langley, Virginia – a garden party which happened to be hosted by a major CIA figure, with the cream of the American military and government in attendance. In July, there were multiple reports both from pilots and ground observers, with both civilian and military radar reporting anomalies in the sky. Then to the horror of the Cold War warriors, the lights appeared over the White House and the Capitol building – the very heart of American government and an entirely restricted airspace. A week later a flight of military jets spent a frustrating night chasing targets that seemed to vanish as they approached, or moved away at impossible speeds. At no point was any structured craft seen – just moving lights and unexplained blips on radar screens. The Washington DC wave has never been fully explained. At the time, the CIA suspected a

Russian stratagem, but this has since been discounted. The most likely – although unproven – cause was the weather effect known as temperature inversion, which can distort normal light sources, such as stars, planets and streetlights, making them appear to move, and also create ghost images or 'angels' on radar screens.

The fact that the most sensitive airspace in the Western world could apparently be penetrated by UFOs (whatever they were) concentrated military and government thinking both in the USA and the UK. In September 1952, just three months after the world-shaking events at Washington, NATO forces undertaking the Operation Mainbrace exercise off eastern England had several UFO encounters, with reports coming in from both RAF jets and an American aircraft carrier. Once again, the suspicion was that these incidents were proof of Soviet secret weapons. Within months the previous free-and-easy atmosphere that had characterised British UFO reports hardened, with military personnel given strict orders not to discuss sightings with the public or the press, and only to report to a specialised intelligence task force at the Air Ministry – the 'UFO desk' as it was later dubbed.

UFO waves rose and fell. There was a major one across several European countries in 1954, and Warminster in Wiltshire became a centre for multiple sightings in the 1960s and 1970s. Florida, California and the American Midwest had several waves, as did Argentina and Mexico. But perhaps the strangest wave of modern times took place in Belgium on 29 November 1989, when 120 reports were received on a single day. Over the next few weeks more sightings came in, with witnesses who included police officers.

The governments of both Belgium and the UK took an official interest, because central and eastern England had experienced its own wave a year earlier – and some of the witness reports were astonishingly similar. Many people reported seeing an enormous flying triangle, sometimes described as being the size of a football field. It was slow moving, silent except for a low humming noise, and lined with bright lights along the edges. The Belgian Air Force, the British Ministry of Defence and other bodies suspected that the craft was an American stealth bomber being secretly tested over European airspace without the permission or knowledge of America's NATO allies. At the time the MOD were convinced the USA was covertly testing a hypersonic craft called the Aurora, and they assiduously collected reports of triangle- and diamond-shaped aircraft (including one from Highland Perthshire in 1990, which may well have been a hoax).

By now, it will be clear, the Cold War was effectively over, and the paranoia it had engendered was being refocused away from the dastardly Russians, to, ironically, the allegedly duplicitous Americans. As it turned out, the Aurora project never existed, being a piece of disinformation disseminated by the US intelligence community, probably to wrong-foot America's enemies. A stealth fighter and a stealth bomber were in development, but these looked nothing like the reported craft, and later investigations showed that no flights by these rare and exotic aircraft had been authorised. (The stealth aircraft were once top secret; now they appear in Hollywood movies.)

The best guess for the identity of the giant triangle was that it was a misidentification of another secret military activity – a mid-air refuelling operation. In this, one or more long-range bombers are connected to a huge tanker plane, the entire set-up surrounded by bright anti-collision lights. The bombers fly behind and to one side of the tanker, creating a 'triangle'. Although the sightings have never been officially explained, the refuelling suggestion is plausible because Western forces were gearing up for the First Gulf War, and may well have been practising long-range bombing and refuelling missions.

The Belgian wave did not stop there, however. As an indication of just how concerned the authorities were, the Belgian Air Force, the airport at Liège, and the premier Belgian UFO group SOBEPS (*Société Belge d'Étude des Phénomènes Spatiaux*) all joined forces to stage a UFO watch in March 1990. At one point fighter planes were launched and one briefly locked on to an unknown radar target. Ground-based radar systems also reported anomalous findings, and some observers on the ground saw strange lights. Unfortunately analysis of the various reports found that none were linked in space and time – the lights were probably atmospheric distortions, and the radar hits may have been caused by 'angels' similar to those involved in the Washington DC wave. Nevertheless, the episode shows that governments and the military can at times take UFOs seriously, even though they are less concerned about alien invasion than they are about intrusions from more earthbound forces.

Some UFO waves seem to be sparked by a cluster of sincere sightings that are then widely reported in the media, leading to a feedback effect in which 'innocent' aerial incidents are mistakenly interpreted as actual

UFOs. In most cases the initial sightings have a prosaic explanation, but by the time this has been worked out and made public, the wave has generated excitement, expectation and a host of false sightings, including hoaxes and mischievous jokes.

IDENTIFIED FLYING OBJECTS (IFOS)

The vast majority of UFOs are in fact Identified Flying Objects or IFOs. More than 250 things in the sky have been found to have caused UFO reports. Some of the most common UFO 'sources' or IFOs are:

- The planet Venus (also known as the Morning Star and the Evening Star, for its close proximity to the sunrise or sunset respectively).

- Other bright stars, sometimes when they are in conjunction with (close to) the brighter planets.

- The Moon (as with Venus and other celestial bodies, the Moon can take on an unusual aspect when low in the sky, viewed through cloud or fog, or glimpsed from a moving vehicle).

- Lenticular (saucer-shaped) clouds and other strange clouds, including those ejected from power stations or created by industrial processes.

- Atmospheric distortions such as the many kinds of mirages.

- Aeroplanes and helicopters.
- Weather balloons, advertising dirigibles, commercial balloons and other lighter-than-air objects.
- Damaged military aircraft ejecting aviation fuel to avoid an on-board explosion (the ejected fuel often ignites, creating a fireball or blaze of light – this was the case in a UFO sighting over Oxfordshire in 1973, the real cause of which was kept secret for 20 years).
- Satellites – especially the International Space Station, which is now, when it is at the right angle, the third brightest object in the sky after the Sun and the Moon.
- Debris from spacecraft or satellites burning up in the atmosphere.
- Meteors.
- Flocks of birds or clouds of insects, particularly during strong sunlight.
- Laser light shows and searchlights, especially when reflective low cloud is present. In some conditions, reflected car headlights can create similar phenomena.
- Chinese or Thai fire lanterns, which are now immensely popular at celebrations and festivals. An internal flame causes the air within a fragile wire and paper frame to expand and 'float' the lantern up into the sky. The orange globes are often seen in slow-moving clusters, giving rise to ideas of 'alien invasion fleets'.

All this being said, a small minority of UFO sightings cannot be so easily explained. This does not mean, of course, that these mysterious sightings are actually of alien spacecraft – it is suggested that there is a whole host of Unidentified Atmospheric Phenomena (UAP) that we do not as yet understand. Our investigations into the natural world at large continue to reveal amazing and bizarre discoveries – in fact, the best place to look for contemporary anomalous and mind-blowing information may not be a magazine devoted to the paranormal, but a peer-reviewed scientific publication such as *The New Scientist* or *Nature*.

SPACE BROTHERS, CONTACTEES AND ALIEN ABDUCTIONS

In 1952, George Adamski became the first human to meet alien beings. He was out UFO-hunting in the Mojave Desert, California, when he was greeted by a tall, blond spaceman from Venus. In later years, he was taken on trips to Mars, Venus and the Moon. He became famous and by default led the 'contactee' movement of the 1950s – a diverse group of Americans who claimed they too had had 'made contact' with extraterrestrials. In contrast to the bug-ugly hostile invaders in the B-movies of the day, the aliens encountered by the contactees were human, good-looking, and concerned about humanity's penchant for pollution, warfare, and nuclear weapons. These 'Space Brothers' were almost universally benign. Even Antonio Villas Boas, a Brazilian farmer who was pulled into a spacecraft by four ETs in 1957, did not complain too much because he was encouraged to make love with an attractive female alien (afterwards she made it clear to him that she would be having his baby in space).

If the aliens of the 1950s were by and large a make-love-not-war bunch, this all changed in the following, darker, decade. The buzzword was no longer 'contact' – now it was 'abduction'. The classic case – indeed, the prototype for many subsequent abduction cases – took place on 19 September 1961. That night, Betty and Barney Hill were returning to their New Hampshire home from a short trip to Canada when they spotted an ominous light that appeared to be following them. With his binoculars Barney saw a discoid craft in the shape of an American pancake, with several figures visible behind a large window. Scared, the couple drove on, only to find their car shaking and beeping as if it was under some sort of remote control. At the same time they both experienced a dream-like sense of disorientation. When they came to, they found they were 35 miles further on, and had lost two hours. Barney felt his genital region was sore, and both knew something awful had happened but they could not remember what. Over the next few weeks Betty had a series of nightmares in which five-foot-tall humanoids carried out medical tests on her, while Barney developed a growth on his groin that required surgery.

Eventually the psychological aftermath of the event – whatever it was – led the couple to seek psychiatric help, which led to sessions of hypnosis in which the night of 19 September was replayed. Both husband and wife described being abducted by aliens and subjected to medical examinations, including sperm samples being extracted from Barney. The psychiatrist concluded that the couple had genuinely experienced something frightening, but that the abduction scenario was a shared delusion rather than the memory of an actual event.

The Hills were educated, respectable, well-liked, and active both in their community and in the civil rights movement (unlike the vast majority of later abductees, Barney was black). The case did not come to light until 1965 when they talked about it at their local church.

The following year, author, John Fuller, wrote a book on the case, called *The Interrupted Journey*. Almost single-handedly the book made alien abduction famous worldwide, and also provided the template for virtually all later abduction scenarios, which typically featured the Hill-related phenomena of 'car stop', 'missing time', 'altered mental states' (sometimes known as the Oz Factor), 'medical examination' and 'post-abduction nightmares or health problems'.

Another example of alien abduction dates from 1975, when forestry worker Travis Walton, from Snowflake, Arizona, was hit by a blue lightning-like beam fired from an ovoid aerial craft. When he awoke he was on board the ship, attended by a group of very small humanoid beings supervised by a taller entity who had the appearance of a human man. Walton was shown a room that seemed to function as a space navigation centre. After some kind of medical examination a mask was slipped over his face and he remembered nothing more until he woke up in a nearby town. In the intervening five days Walton had been officially missing, with a massive search being conducted by the local authorities. Walton passed a lie detector test and appeared thoroughly sincere in his descriptions of his experience. At one time, this was one of the most famous abduction cases and it was made into a Hollywood movie, *Fire From The Sky*, in 1993. Subsequent investigators have not questioned Walton's sincerity, but have pointed out that he had an abiding interest in science fiction and UFO reports, and that a television movie of the Betty and Barney Hill case was shown just before the alleged incident. It is possible that Walton had a genuinely distressing experience, possibly even being really hit by lightning, and the imaginative or fantasy-prone nature of his personality did the rest.

Some 6,000 alleged abduction cases have been recorded since the 1961 original. Over time, descriptions of the experience have become both more elaborate and even darker, with accounts of the forced removal of eggs from ovaries, probes inserted into all orifices, the implantation of 'tracking' devices in the skin, and even 'walk-ins', in which small, frail aliens 'walk inside' obese people so that they are protected by the layers of fat.

Yet outside the experiences that people relate, there is no evidence for alien abductions – no abductee has provided alien DNA, for instance. In addition, whereas once upon a time abductees reported meeting a whole range of different aliens (from small elf- or goblin-like creatures to noble or attractive Caucasian humanoids, stick-thin 'technicians' and even robot-organic hybrids), since the 1980s virtually all descriptions conform to a standard pattern, the large-eyed and egg-shaped 'Greys'. Greys were first popularised by Whitley Streiber's widely publicised book *Communion*, and have since colonised TV shows, films, magazine covers and T-shirts. It seems likely that people are now reporting Grey-like beings simply because that is what they *expect* aliens to look like – an example of what ufologists call 'cultural tracking', in which UFO reports are influenced by information disseminated in popular culture and the mass media. *The X-Files*, *Close Encounters of the Third Kind*, *Independence Day* and other works of entertainment have all been seen to shape the way witnesses describe UFOs and aliens.

Most of the abduction cases are from the USA, and sceptics point to the widespread American use of hypnosis to 'recover' supposed lost memories. As has been shown with some cases of alleged child sexual abuse where the therapists have an agenda, such attempts at 'recovering' suppressed experiences may in fact simply invent the memories, and it is suggested that many 'abduction memories' are merely fantasies created by the hypnosis itself. It may be significant that reports of alien abductions are far lower in the UK, where the UFO research community eschews the use of hypnotic regression.

It has been suggested that the matrix of bizarre psychological and physiological states that can affect anyone under unusual conditions may be at play here, from what are called 'fantasy-prone personalities' to waking dreams, sleep paralysis, dream or fugue states, and undetected transient temporal lobe epilepsy. In truth, any one of us can have an 'altered state' experience under the right circumstances; alien abduction scenarios may simply be a way of using a template from popular culture to channel these anomalous mental states.

The most mysterious thing in the universe is not 'out there' in space: it is the human brain.

OTHER ENCOUNTERS WITH ALIENS

Most UFO sightings are little more than what has been termed 'Lights In The Sky' or LITS. In a LITS incident, no structured craft or anything solid is seen, just one or more lights. A minority of sightings report what appears to be a nuts-and-bolts craft. Although witnesses describe a huge variety of shapes, some forms are more common than others. Saucers were popular in the 1940s and 1950s, while similar disc-shaped craft are still reported to this day. Cigar-shapes were common in the 1950s and 1960s, while diamonds and triangles have been on the rise since the 1980s. A report from Dundee in the 1990s even described a giant Zeppelin-like craft, harking back to the mystery airships of a century earlier.

But witness reports are ten a penny, and easily dismissed. Photographs of UFOs can be (and have been) faked. For those ufologists who ascribe to the ETH, the 'holy grail' of their quest is solid physical proof of an alien spaceship or an extraterrestrial being. For some, two British cases tantalisingly hint at that proof. The first, dubbed the 'Welsh Roswell', took place in the Berwyn Mountains of North Wales on 23 January 1974. An explosion and a loud rumbling sound, accompanied by a series of rapidly moving bright lights, awakened inhabitants of the nearby village of Llandrillo. Out of the ensuing confusion, and exaggerated by the presence of the police and the army warning people to keep away from what was believed to be a crashed aircraft, there evolved a bizarre belief: that this was the crash site of an extraterrestrial spacecraft. The story grew slowly, but, given an impetus by the now-established Roswell mythology, it soon sprouted arms and legs in the familiar form of alien bodies, advanced ET technology, a secret military operation and (of course) a cover-up.

In some ways, however, what really appeared to have happened is just as bizarre. Researchers have established that a minor earthquake took place at the same time as a bolide meteor shower was lighting up the sky. Bolides are exceptionally bright meteors and are often mistaken for UFOs. The moving lights have been attributed to poachers out illegally 'lamping' on the mountain at night. This series of coincidences demonstrate that at times, reality can be just as weird as anything dreamt up by the human imagination.

The second, and even weirder, British case is known as the 'Livingston Incident'. On the night of 9 November 1979, a forestry worker called Bob Taylor claimed to have encountered three spherical hovering objects in the middle of the woods near Livingston, just off the M8 motorway west of Edinburgh. Taylor was walking through the woods when he emerged into a clearing where he beheld a giant sphere, about 20 feet across, made of a dark metallic material. As he looked on, two smaller, spiked spheres dropped from the main one and rolled towards him. Attaching themselves to his trouser legs, they drew him towards the main sphere, where he was assaulted by an acrid stench that made him choke and finally lose consciousness. When he awoke, he found himself alone and unable to speak. He staggered home, where his wife called the police. Though his tale was incredible, they investigated because he was a man of previously reliable character, and the working assumption, based on the evidence of tears on his clothes, was that he had been assaulted. The police found strange marks, like ladders, on the ground where Taylor said he had seen the spheres, along with holes that were consistent with marks that could have been made by 'spiked spheres'. Despite extensive investigation the trail went cold, though the police case remains open. For the rest of his life Taylor maintained that his experience had been real.

One suggestion is that something startled Taylor, prompting an epileptic fit. However, he had never experienced epilepsy before or after the incident. Was this then a close encounter of the third kind – the kind where humans meet aliens? Many ufologists believe it is the only explanation and it remains one of the most puzzling cases in the annals of UFO studies.

Another celebrated European case was the utterly surreal incident near the rural Finnish village of Imjärvi in 1970. Esko Viljo and Aarno Heinonen were out skiing on a clear winter's night when they encountered a small disc descending in a luminous red-grey cloud. A beam of light issued from the disc, revealing a 3-foot-high figure dressed in green clothing, pointed hat, boots and gloves. It had claw-like fingers, a hooked nose and distinctively pointed ears. In other words, it resembled the goblins or trolls of Scandinavian folklore. The figure was carrying a box, which emitted coloured sparks and a blinding beam of light. The bizarre alien was then retracted back into the craft, which disappeared in a flash of light. Heinonen found that the arm and leg that had been facing the silent explosion were paralysed. When they finally struggled off the snow slopes, Viljo having to support his friend, both men were exhibiting severe symptoms. Viljo's skin was red and raw, as if he had been out in strong sunlight, and his face and eyes were puffy and swollen. Heinonen, meanwhile, suffered severe urinary infections, migraine, nausea and psychological problems that kept him off work for several years. Although psychosomatic illnesses are not unknown among abductees, the scale of the damage to the pair suggested a real physical cause. In many ways the men appeared to have been subjected to radiation poisoning, but no radioactive readings were found from their clothing or the site of the encounter. No convincing explanation has been forthcoming for the Imjärvi incident.

ANCIENT ASTRONAUTS

1968 saw the appearance of one of the most epochal books on extraterrestrials, Erich von Däniken's *Chariots of the Gods?* Extensively serialised in newspapers, the book went on to sell a staggering 40 million copies. Von Däniken's central thesis was that aliens had visited earth on many occasions in the distant past, gifting knowledge and technology to early civilisations. In return the humans recorded the visits of these 'gods' in their monuments and art. The Swiss researcher compiled examples of representations of 'spacemen' from archaeological sites around the world, from Stonehenge, Egypt and India to the Mayas of Mexico, the Incas of Peru, and various islands in the Pacific. At one level, it was a revelation, tapping into the 1960s zeitgeist, the Space Race, and matching similar themes elsewhere, such as the 'aliens created humanity' idea central to the book and film *2001: A Space Odyssey*. Certainly *Chariots of the Gods?* inspired a generation to explore 'alternative archaeology', earth mysteries and other countercultural realms. But taken another way, it was pure bunkum.

Von Däniken's main problem was that he had what is known as an *idée fixe* (a fixed idea) and was unwilling to contemplate alternative suggestions, such as the fact that human art is often complex, frequently non-naturalistic and filled with meanings that are important to the culture at the time – meanings that can be obscure to us in modern times. If he saw a Mayan carving of a distorted humanoid surrounded by strange shapes, to him that was a direct representation of an alien in its space capsule. In vain did archaeologists argue that such nonrealistic carvings were the way the Mayans conventionally depicted their rulers or deities. Similar arguments were raised against many of von Däniken's other claims, from 'UFO landing sites' to alien Pharoahs. One of the most popular claims for early documentation of an alien encounter focused on the Old Testament visions of Ezekial. The prophet described an aerial apparition of four winged creatures:

> 'In the midst of the living creatures was something that looked like burning coals of fire, like torches moving to and fro, like a flash of lightning ... I saw a wheel upon the earth beside the living creatures, one for each of the four ... their construction being as it were a wheel within a wheel. When they went, they went in any of their four directions without turning as they went. The four wheels rims were so high that they were dreadful and their rims

were full of eyes round about. And when
the living creatures went, the wheels went
beside them; and when the living creatures
rose from the earth, the wheels rose.'

According to von Däniken's literal interpretation,
this was an alien's ground exploration vehicle, or
possibly a kind of amphibious helicopter. Academics
steeped in the Biblical world however, have convincingly
demonstrated that Ezekial's vision is couched in the
symbolic language of the time, and the entire passage
is a coded description of the powerful nations of the
Middle East at the time, all ruled over by the Jewish
god Jehovah. Once again, cultural context reveals the
rich symbolism of the art, as against von Däniken's
reductive hypothesis that anything ancient and strange
must be evidence of alien interference in the human
past. In many ways, the ancient astronauts idea does a
disservice to the skills and intelligence of our ancestors:
we didn't need aliens to teach us how to build stone
circles or pyramids, because we were already smart
enough to do these things ourselves. These days von
Däniken's claims have less currency than they once
did, although he has published a successful series of
similarly themed books, and he has a *Chariots of the
Gods* theme park in Switzerland.

CROP CIRCLES

In the summer of 1978, strange flattened areas began
to appear in the crop fields of southern England,
especially Wiltshire and Hampshire. Initially roughly
circular or oval in shape, they soon started to appear

in ever more complex forms. As aerial photographs of the increasingly fantastic shapes were published in the press, the numbers and elaborate geometry of the shapes grew. By the mid-1980s crop circles were an expected part of the British summer season, taking their place in the calendar alongside cricket matches and music festivals – and, perhaps not coincidentally, many of the circle designs echoed fractal patterns and other psychedelic imagery popular with the emerging rave culture. Each year the designs became more ambitious, more beautiful, and more puzzling. Soon foreign visitors were combining visits to the stone circles of Avebury and Stonehenge with trips on the lookout for crop circles; it was a genuinely new British phenomenon.

Crop circles quickly attracted all sorts of notions as to their origin. The most popular suggestions were:

- Freak winds.
- Fungal infection leading to the weakening of the stalks, which then bent in the wind.
- Ball lightning.
- Unknown electromagnetic effects, possibly connected to fluctuations in the earth's magnetic field.
- Unknown atmospheric phenomena.
- A 'plasma vortex' – an entirely hypothetical but scientifically plausible cloud of ionized atmospheric gas caused by lightning interacting with the earth's magnetic field. The complex patterns of the crop circles are created when the vortex strikes the

ground and are thought to mirror other elaborate shapes found in nature, such as the astonishing complexity of a snowflake.

- Secret military technology such as microwave weapons or blasts from satellites.
- UFO landing sites.
- Creations by extraterrestrials seeking to deliver a message to mankind.

Then in 1991 a pair of amateur artists, Doug Bower and Dave Chorley, came forward and claimed that they had created the majority of the circles – and even demonstrated how they did it. Doug and Dave, as they were known, caused a sensation. For most observers, that was it, game over – the circles were a hoax. For others who were more committed to one of the hypotheses listed above, they believed that Doug and Dave could not have made *all* the circles. Even when it became clear that the prankster duo had inspired an entire generation of covert circle-makers to produce 'temporary landscape art', some people still clung to the idea that at least some of the circles had a paranormal origin.

And, indeed, it is difficult to see how some of the larger patterns could have been made undetected in a single summer's night – since Doug and Dave's day, circles have appeared that are almost a sixth of a mile across, with hundreds of swirls, curlicues and other patterns. On the other hand, it never pays to underestimate the sneaky intelligence of human beings, and perhaps the bigger circles are the work of a collective numbering in the dozens, with each individual tasked with creating just one part of the whole.

Then there is a curious case from 1678, the 'Mowing Devil', in which a field of oats in Hertfordshire was said to have been cut down in concentric circles by a supernatural force – which suggests that crop circles may have a deep ancestry, and that the simpler ones may indeed be created by natural action. Or, if you are so minded, you could read the 17th-century account as evidence that crop-molesting aliens have been with us for several hundred years.

The idea that 'crop circles are made by aliens' has been exploited in on-screen entertainment such as the TV drama *Dark Skies* and the film *Signs*. And the more crop circles are depicted in this way, the more both their shapes and the belief that they are communications from ETs become part of the 'background radiation' of popular culture. Although some people think that the golden age of crop circles was in the 1990s and the 2000s, examples still appear in the English countryside every summer. And they are still wonderful, still weird and still a bit puzzling.

THE MIN MIN LIGHTS

'Suddenly I realised it was not a car light – it remained in one bulbous ball instead of dividing into the two headlights, which it should have done as it came closer; it was too green-glary for an acetylene light; it floated too high for any car; there was something eerie about it. The light came on, floating as airily as a bubble, moving with comparative slowness ... I should estimate now that it was moving at about

10 mph and anything from 5 to 10 feet above the ground ... Its size, I would say, at an approximate guess, would be about that of a new-risen moon. That light and I passed each other, going in opposite directions. I kept an eye on it while it was passing, and I'd say it was about 200 yards off when suddenly it just faded and died away. It did not go out with a snap – its vanishing was more like the gradual fading of the wires in an electric bulb.'

That was the experience of rancher Henry Lamond in 1922, in Western Queensland. Even today this outback area of Australia is a relatively remote, vast flat expanse of largely nothing: a perfect landscape for an enduring mystery. There was once a town here called Min Min, and the Min Min Lights still haunt the area, attracting everyone from ghost hunters to UFO enthusiasts. Also known as 'Dead Men's Campfire' or the 'Debil Debil', the lights were first reported by European settlers in 1838, and given names familiar from British supernatural folklore, such as Will o' the Wisp and Jack o' Lantern. Aborigines described the lights as powerful sorcerers on their travels, or ancestor spirits wandering the landscape. The lights vary in colour from white to orange, and in size from a lantern-sized glow to large balls. Sometimes they follow humans, sometimes they move away from them, and sometimes they act independently, moving in straight lines or oscillating back and forth. Almost always they keep close to the ground. The Min Min Lights have been observed by so many different people that they are regarded as genuine phenomena, and these days tourists can go on 'Min Min' hunts.

In the 1950s, the most popular idea about the lights was that they were the spirit of a notorious bushranger who had been killed in a local drinking den (an elaboration of this ascribed the sheer number of lights to the wandering spirits of the murderer's victims). By the late 1970s, the emphasis had very much shifted to a UFO explanation, with the most popular idea being that the lights were small alien probes operating under remote control from a 'mothership' elsewhere (a related idea conceived the alien base as being beneath Ayers Rock, the iconic red-coloured desert mountain honoured as 'Uluru' by the Aboriginal people of Australia).

Scientists, however, have long suspected that the lights are rooted in the natural environment. Ball lightning (see page 65) and geophysically generated electromagnetic effects (see 'earthlights' on page 66) have been suggested, along with phosphorescence (marsh-gas) and wind-blown mists or dust clouds. In 2003, optics specialist Professor Jack Pettigrew offered an explanation based on the *Fata Morgana* – a 'superior mirage' in which an image of an object far below the horizon is seen above the horizon, in a 'superior position'. Pettigrew tested the idea by having a car parked with its headlights on, and then moving beyond the horizon – and, as if by magic, Min Min Lights appeared at the second location. When the car's headlights were switched off, the Min Min faded away.

The *Fata Morgana*, by the way, is named after King Arthur's sister Morgana le Fey, who was said to be able to levitate objects through her magic.

UNIDENTIFIED SUBMERSIBLE OBJECTS (USOS)

The Puerto Rico Trench is one of the deepest parts of the ocean floor, and one of the world's hot spots for sightings of what are called Unidentified Submersible Objects or USOs. In a sense, USOs are the underwater equivalent of UFOs – they respond as moving metallic objects to sonar, move at speeds and perform manoeuvres that are impossible for conventional craft, and operate at depths that would crush a normal submarine. Even stranger, some USOs are said to break the surface, fly or hover for a short period, and then return beneath the waves. USOs have been reported over several decades by various navies from around the world, including those of the USA and the USSR/Russia.

USO sightings are, not surprisingly, far rarer than those of UFOs, and so the literature is much less extensive, with no reliable definitive analysis of the phenomenon. The suggestions put forward are therefore also more tentative. Starting with the obvious, some cases could result from observer error or equipment malfunction. What have been logged as 'craft' could conceivably be marine animals, such as giant squid or schools of dolphins. Perhaps they are indeed craft, but their origin lies with the testing of secret experimental weapons by the US military. Freak weather conditions may be a factor, as could little-understood underwater electromagnetic activity, possibly associated with submarine volcanoes or earthquakes. Moving into the more mystical realm, believers in the Atlantis myth suggest USOs are in fact submersibles powered by advanced Atlantean technology and operating from secret subsea locations. But for some ufologists, the answer lies in the extraterrestrial hypothesis. Here, the Puerto Rico Trench location is the key factor, for Puerto Rico is home to the giant Arecibo radio telescope, which, among other things, is part of SETI, the Search for Extraterrestrial Intelligence. Arecibo has transmitted radio messages into space, in the hope that they might be received by technological extraterrestrial civilisations. For believers, the aliens have followed the messages back to their point of origin, and have set up bases in the ocean depths so they can monitor goings on at Arecibo.

ARE 'THEY' HERE?

Despite more than six decades of intense global interest in all aspects of the UFO/aliens subject, no-one has produced even the slightest reliable hint that extraterrestrials are among us. Along the way, we have learned a great deal about the workings of the human brain and our perceptions, uncovered hitherto unknown atmospheric phenomena, and expanded our knowledge of the stranger side of nature, from meteors to mirages. And the field has produced innumerable alien-related films and TV series – the impact of which should not be underestimated, as the nature of sightings often 'tracks' images seen in these powerful fiction media.

But are 'they' actually here? In our current state of knowledge we cannot state that extraterrestrial life actually exists, although there are strong hopes that traces of life will soon be found on Mars, or one of the moons of Jupiter or Saturn. In addition, more than

500 planets have been detected in other solar systems, of which around 150 are 'earth-like' – that is, they are small and rocky and are at the right distance from their star to support temperatures that allow liquid water to form, water currently being regarded as one of the prerequisites of life. All these planets have been discovered in just the past few years, in what could be regarded as our galactic backyard. As our telescope and deep-space technologies improve, we will no doubt find many more planets – there could easily be millions just in our own galaxy, never mind amongst the trillions of other stars. So it is a racing certainty that life exists outside our own little planet – we just haven't found it yet.

But it is a big leap from thinking we might find bacteria on Mars to suggesting that there are intelligent races out there, beings who have not only developed propulsion technology but have worked out how to cross the unimaginably vast distances of space. And it is an even bigger leap to think that any such ultra-intelligent voyagers would be interested in us, in our tiny backwater of the universe.

The best guess, then, is that our toxic obsession with alien visitors is not about 'them' but about 'us'. Extraterrestrials are the products of our hopes, our fears, our fixations and our fantasies. They belong to the realms of sociology, psychology and human physiology. Of course, all of this will be instantly disproved if the Mothership lands on the White House lawn tomorrow. But most likely the aliens are here simply because we are the most imaginative and weirdest creatures on our planet.

BIBLIOGRAPHY

Alexander, Marc *Enchanted Britain* (Arthur Barker; London, 1981)

Arment, Chad *The Historical Bigfoot* (Coachwhip Publications; Landisville, Pennsylvania, 2006)

Arnold, Neil *Monster! The A-Z of Zooform Phenomena* (CFZ Press; Woolfardisworthy, 2007)

Ashe, Geoffrey *Mythology of The British Isles* (Methuen; London, 1992)

Binns, Ronald *The Loch Ness Mystery Solved* (W.H. Allen; London, 1983)

Bird, Christopher *The Divining Hand: The 500-Year-Old Mystery of Dowsing* (Whitford Press; Atglen, Pennsylvania, 1993)

Bord, Janet and Colin *Modern Mysteries of Britain: 100 Years of Strange Events* (Grafton Books; London, 1987)

Broughton, Richard S. 'Memory, Emotion, and the Receptive Psi Process' in *The Journal of Parapsychology* (Vol. 70, Fall 2006)

Budden, Albert *Electric UFOs: Fireballs, Electromagnetics and Abnormal States* (Blandford; London, 1998)

Cadman, S. Parkes *The Three Religious Leaders of Oxford and Their Movements: John Wycliffe, John Wesley, John Henry Newman* (Macmillan; New York, 1916)

Campbell, Steuart *The Loch Ness Monster: The Evidence* (Aberdeen University Press; Aberdeen, 1991)

Carrington, Hereward & Nandor Fodor *The Story of the Poltergeist Down the Centuries* (Rider & Co.; London, 1953)

Castleden, Rodney *Ancient British Hill Figures* (S.B. Publications; Seaford, 2000)

Chippendale, Christopher *Stonehenge Complete* (Thames & Hudson; London, 2004)

Crowe, Catherine *The Night Side of Nature* (Wordsworth Editions/The Folklore Society; Ware/London, 2000 [1848])

Däniken, Erich von *Chariots of the Gods?* (Souvenir Press; London, 1990 [1968])

Devereux, Paul *Earthlights: Towards an Explanation of the UFO Enigma* (Turnstone Press; Wellingborough, 1992)

Devereux, Paul *Shamanism and the Mystery Lines: 'Ley Lines', Spirit Paths and Out-of-Body Travel* (Quantum; Slough, 2001)

Devereux, Paul *Spirit Roads: An Exploration of Otherworldly Routes* (Collins & Brown; London, 2007)

Dinsdale, Tim *The Leviathans* (Routledge & Kegan Paul; London, 1966)

Ellis, Peter Beresford *A Brief History of the Druids* (Constable & Robinson; London, 2002)

Fuller, John G. *The Interrupted Journey: Two Lost Hours Aboard a Flying Saucer* (Souvenir Press; London, 1980)

Gauld, Alan & A.D. Cornell, *Poltergeists* (Routledge & Kegan Paul; London, 1979)

Geoffrey of Monmouth & Lewis Thorpe (ed.) *The History of the Kings of Britain* (Penguin; Harmondsworth, 2004)

Gould, Charles *Mythical Monsters* (W. H. Allen & Co.; London, 1886)

Grey, Affleck *Legends of the Cairngorms* (Mainstream Publishing; Edinburgh, 1992)

Hallowell, Michael J. & Darren W. Ritson *The South Shields Poltergeist* (The History Press; Stroud, 2008)

Hancock, Graham *Supernatural – Meetings with the Ancient Teachers of Mankind* (Century; London, 2005)

Harrison, Paul *The Encyclopaedia of the Loch Ness Monster* (Robert Hale; London, 1999)

Hutton, Ronald *The Pagan Religions of the British Isles: Their Nature and Legacy* (Basil Blackwell; Oxford, 1991)

Kaku, Michio *Hyperspace: A Scientific Odyssey through Parallel Universes, Time Warps, and the Tenth Dimension* (Oxford University Press; Oxford, 1995)

McCue, Peter 'Theories Of Haunting: A Critical Overview' in *The Journal of the Society for Psychical Research* (Vol. 66, 2002)

McEwan, Graham J. *Sea Serpents, Sailors and Sceptics* (Routledge & Kegan Paul; London, 1978)

McGovern, Una (ed.) *Chambers Dictionary of the Unexplained* (Chambers Harrap; Edinburgh, 2007)

Mackal, Roy P. *A Living Dinosaur? In Search of Mokole-Mbembe* (E. J. Brill; Leiden, 1987)

Marshall, Steve, George Currie and Pete Glastonbury 'Investigation of a "Sun Roll" Effect in Relation to Silbury Hill' in *Time and Mind: The Journal of Archaeology, Consciousness and Culture* (Vol. 3, Issue 3, November 2010)

Martinez-Taboas, A. 'An appraisal of the role of aggression and the central nervous system in RSPK agents' in *The Journal of the American Society for Psychical Research* (Vol. 78, 1984)

Michell, John & Bob Rickard *Unexplained Phenomena: A Rough Guide Special* (Rough Guides; London, 2000)

Newman, Paul *Lost Gods of Albion: The Chalk Hill-Figures of Britain* (Sutton Publishing; Stroud, 1999)

Oudemans, A. C. *The Great Sea-Serpent: An Historical and Critical Treatise* (Luzac & Co.; London, 1892)

Piggott, Stuart *Ancient Britons and the Antiquarian Imagination* (Thames & Hudson; London, 1990)

Playfair, Guy Lyon *This House is Haunted: An Investigation into the Enfield Poltergeist* (Souvenir Press; London, 1980)

Price, Harry *Poltergeist: Tales of the Supernatural* (Bracken Books; London 1993, (1945)).

Price, Harry & R. S. Lambert *The Haunting of Cashen's Gap* (Methuen; London, 1936)

Randall, John L. *Psychokinesis: A Study of Paranormal Forces through the Ages* (Souvenir Press; London, 1982)

Randi, James *James Randi: Psychic Investigator* (Boxtree; London, 1991)

Randles, Jenny & Peter Hough *Spontaneous Human Combustion* (Bantam Books; London, 1993)

Rhine, Louisa *Hidden Channels of the Mind* (Sloane Associates; Clifton, New Jersey, 1961)

Roberts, Andy 'Ley lines to oblivion' in *Northern Earth* (No. 55 [1993])

Rogo, D. Scott *Beyond Reality: The Role Unseen Dimensions Play in Our Lives* (The Aquarian Press; Wellingborough, 1990)

Rogo, D. Scott *The Poltergeist Experience* (The Aquarian Press; Wellingborough, 1990 [1979])

Roll, William G. *The Poltergeist* (Paraview; New York, 2004 (1972))

Roll, William G. 'Poltergeists' in Wolman, B. B. (ed.) *Handbook of Parapsychology*, (Van Nostrand Reinhold; New York, 1977)

Romer, C. 'The poverty of theory: notes on the investigation of spontaneous cases' in *The Journal of the Society for Psychical Research* (Vol. 61, 1996)

Ronson, Jon *The Men Who Stare at Goats* (Picador; London, 2005)

Schwartz, Gary E., Linda G. S. Russick, Lonnie A. Nelson & Christopher Barentsen 'Accuracy and Replicability of Anomalous After-Death Communication across Highly Skilled Mediums' in *The Journal of the Society for Psychical Research (*Vol. 66, 2001)

Shine, Adrian *Loch Ness* (Loch Ness Project; Drumnadrochit, 2006)

Shuker, Karl P. N. *In Search of Prehistoric Survivors* (Blandford; London, 1995)

Smiles, Sam *The Image of Antiquity: Ancient Britain and the Romantic Imagination* (Yale University Press; New Haven and London, 1994)

Stommel, Henry *Lost Islands: The story of islands that have vanished from nautical charts* (University of British Colombia Press; Vancouver, 1984)

Sullivan, Danny *Ley Lines: A Comprehensive Guide to Alignments* (Piatkus; London, 1999)

Watkins, Alfred *The Old Straight Track* (Abacus; London, 1994 [1925])

Williamson, Tom and Liz Bellamy *Ley Lines in Question* (World's Work; Tadworth, 1983)

Wilson, Colin *Mysteries* (Granada; London, 1979)

Wilson, Colin *Poltergeist! A Study in Destructive Haunting* (New English Library; Sevenoaks, 1981)